POP

Fathering in a modern-day world

Willy Bowles

Forewords by
Dr. Sam Huddleston
Banning Liebscher

Addendum John Withers

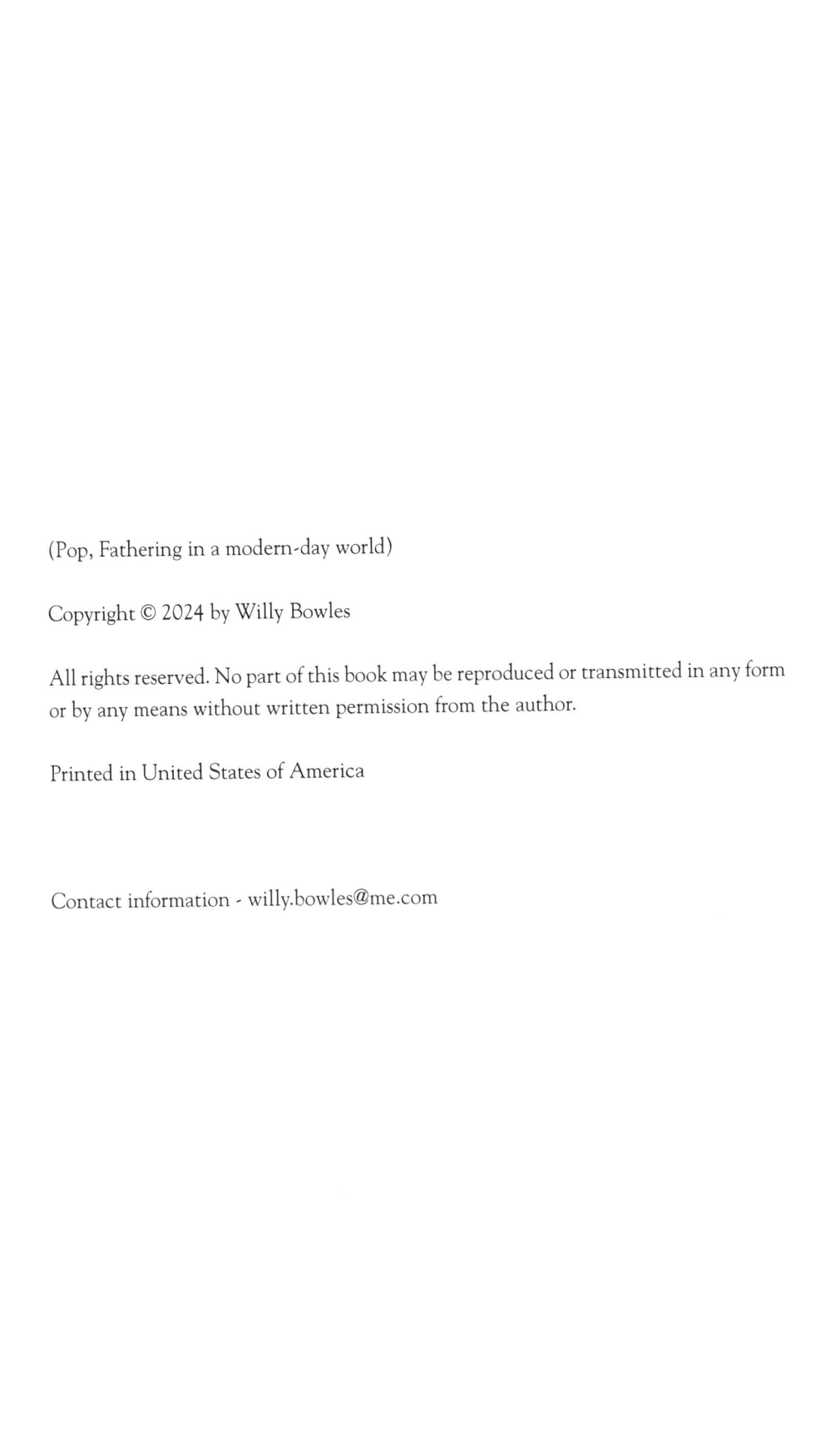

(Pop, Fathering in a modern-day world)

Copyright © 2024 by Willy Bowles

All rights reserved. No part of this book may be reproduced or transmitted in any form or by any means without written permission from the author.

Printed in United States of America

Contact information - willy.bowles@me.com

Table of Contents

Foreword: Dr Sam Huddleston v
Foreword: Banning Liebscher vii
Dedication ix
Introduction xi
In their own words 1
Why we need fathers today more than ever 5
A skunk in the house 11
Let's Go Fishing 17
Parenting fails, and I'm sorry 21
It's a Dance! 25
Core Values 31
Calm in the Storm 35
The Greatest Coaching Talk of All Time 41
Influence 45
Times are changing 51
Legacy 59
When You Are Ready For a Change, Change will Be Ready For You 61
Confessions of a Single Parent (Just for fun!) 69
Encouragement 71
Tear out promises 73
Special Thanks 89

Foreword: Dr Sam Huddleston

I'm frequently asked to write an endorsement for a new book. Often my schedule won't allow it. As my friend Willy is so transparent in his writing, let me be so now. Sometimes I ask my admin to read the manuscript, write something up for me to edit and sign off on. But with this book, <u>Pops</u>, written by my brother and friend, Willy, I read the entire manuscript in one sitting. I felt motivated, inspired, challenged, and encouraged in so many ways. It has helped me be a better grandparent to my 13 grandchildren, although the book is not written for grandfathers. This book not only tells a story but gives wonderful, practical advice on how to be a parent. Willy says he wasn't a stepparent. He is a man who, "stepped" in and became a "parent" to over 100 foster children. He shares how their lives were transformed by the love of Christ living through them as a couple. It is incredibly real. If you are expecting to read a story that is sad, this is not that book. Nor is it a book about guilt.

If you want a book that is religious, this is not it. But if you want to read a book that will help you as a parent, a man, or a woman, then read this book. This book is not filled with theory. It is filled with wisdom that Willy and his first wife were graced to live out with their young family. That's right, his first wife. I have known Willy for over 2 decades. From our first meeting to this day, I truly enjoy being around him. Whether it is in his home eating an incredible meal that he cooked, or riding for hours in a car, I have never been bored with my friend. You will read about pain and disappointment, all of which are covered by the grace and love of our almighty God. I write this endorsement about a dear friend to a reader I believe will soon become a friend of Willy as well. I love you, brother. Your words are healing and will help all who read them. I know it has taken you a long time to write this book. Healing can be that way. Thanks for sharing your life with all of us. You are loved by many, big fella. I am glad to be one of the many.

Dr. Samuel Huddleston
Assistant Superintendent - Assemblies of God Northern CA & NV
Executive Presbyter - Assemblies of God USA
Author of Five Years to Life & Grand Slam

Foreword: Banning Liebscher

The great need of the hour—both in the body of Christ and in the world—is fathers. We have a generation of young people who have grown up in broken, dysfunctional, and often fatherless homes. Not coincidentally, this generation has also been walking away from the church in large numbers.

The church is supposed to be a family. But if this family is just as broken, dysfunctional, and fatherless as the rest of the world, we don't have anything different to offer an orphaned generation, who despite being hesitant with organized religion, are starving for identity, purpose, and spiritual and relational connection.

There is no denying the essential role that good fathers play in the home. Good mothers are just as essential, but they provide different things. Fathers create safety, identity, purpose, and courage in the hearts of their children.

To do that, of course, they must be engaged and present with their kids and willing to walk with them through the messiness of growing up. It's not always fun and almost never glamorous being in the trenches with your kids, but that's where the powerful, unconditional love of a father gets expressed. That's where they learn, "My dad loves me and believes in me no matter how many times I mess up."

Genuine discipleship looks more like a family then it does a classroom. God is calling us to walk with people on the long and often messy journey of learning how to follow Jesus and allow Him to heal and transform their lives. But just like parenting, it's through walking with people that we demonstrate the Father's heart for them. Sermons, conferences, and encounters with the presence of God are needed, but it is in the day-in, day-out process of discipleship that we are re-parented into a secure identity as sons and daughters of God.

Willy Bowles is a pastor and father who has spent his life walking with broken people through the messiness of life and loving them unconditionally. The beauty of Willy's life and his message is the revelation that the greatest thing one could ever do is pour themselves out for others. Any man can become a father if he chooses to walk alongside them, engage with their life, and love them unconditionally. The stories Willy shares in this book are honest, vulnerable, relatable, and ultimately encouraging to every man who recognizes the massive need for fathers today and wants to step into this holy calling.

As someone who has dedicated my life to believing God for revival in the church and a harvest in the nations, I believe Willy is doing one of the most important things we can do to prepare for an orphan generation to turn to Jesus—raising up fathers who are ready and willing to love them, walk with them, and show them the Father, just as Jesus did with His disciples. Just before He went to the cross, Jesus told them, "You did not choose Me, but I chose you and appointed you that you should go and bear fruit, and that your fruit should remain, that whatever you ask the Father in My name He may give you" (John 15:16). Jesus was talking about the people who would be transformed as the disciples walked with them, just as they were transformed by walking with Jesus. Transformed people are the fruit that remains. There is nothing more important, more impactful, or more glorious we can do with our lives than to pour them into the life of others. This is how we will leave a legacy, not just for our generation, but for eternity.

Banning Liebscher
Founder | Lead Pastor
Jesus Culture Pastor

Dedication

This book is dedicated to my Pop. Although he will never read these pages as he passed away on May 30th, 2014, I know he would love every page and encourage me to continue being a writer. After all, he supported me in every dream I ever had. Pop, you were my best friend, my role model, my hero, and the one man I always wanted to be like. You were the most generous man I have ever known. You were strong and loving and always took care of your family. You worked long hours, longer than you should have, but you never missed a game. You were always the one man I knew who had my back. I will never stop loving you. You were my dad, but I called you Pop. Thanks for being the best Pop ever. I will always love and miss you.

Introduction

We live in a fantastic world. According to Steven Pinker and his book *Enlightenment Now*, we have more peace on the planet than at any other time in history. We have less famine, disease, and suffering than humanity has ever experienced. We have a medical community that is on the cutting edge of science, and I believe it will not be long before we hear the words, "We have a cure for cancer." We live in a time when you can pick up a phone that fits in your pocket and make a video call to somebody on the other side of the planet, and it looks and sounds pretty darn good. We live in a world where your car will drive itself, and a little robot vacuums your floors when you're not home. We have the internet, a place/thing almost endless in its capabilities. We are truly living in a day and age that 30 years ago was nothing but science fiction. Yes, our world is getting better and not worse, but we still have our problems. Today, more than ever, we need fathers. I have heard that "a lack of fathers is the cause of inner-city problems." I have also heard that "a lack of fathers is an epidemic in the black community." I'm afraid I have to disagree with those statements. I think the lack of fathers is an epidemic in all communities. I am writing this book because I have seen first-hand what not having fathers does to children and how those children respond when given a father. I am writing to dads everywhere who have stepped up and taken on the role of a father. Dads, we only have one life to live and one chance to do it right. Love well! If there is anything I have ever regretted while being a father, it was those times when I reacted out of anger and not love. As a father, our primary goal needs to be love, and I am not talking just about a love that provides. Yes, being a provider is an act of love, and we will talk about it and what that means in this book. But I have spoken with many dads who tell me, "Of course, I love my kids. They are why I get up and go to work every day". That is awesome, but I am talking about something different. I am talking about letting your kids see your love, feel it, and know your love on a level greater than providing a roof over their heads and food on the table.

You are not supposed to be alone, so stop acting like it. The Marlboro man is a myth. For those not old enough to remember what I'm talking about, the Marlboro man was a character in a cigarette commercial. Yes, they used to advertise cigarettes on TV. He was pictured as a man sitting on a horse smoking a cigarette. A Marlboro cigarette! He was alone, strong, and independent. He never showed emotion for any reason and certainly never cried. He was the ideal picture of a man's man, but that man is a myth. The Marlboro man doesn't really exist, and if he does, he is not very happy. He is constantly conflicted with this persona, and when the Marlboro Man rides away on his horse, he is by himself. The Marlboro man is alone; he doesn't have family, kids, or relationships. Don't be like the Marlboro man. A man loves, and a man loves passionately. Hug your kids, kiss your kids, hug your wife, kiss your wife, love those around you, and let your children see you loving those around you. My memories of my father are of the times he loved others. To be a man doesn't need to be hard, tough, or stern. Yes, there may be times for all those emotions and actions, but those should be rare moments uncharacteristic of who you are and how you act. Your kids will follow you if they know you love them. Your kids will be successful if they know you love them.

Love conquers all. There is no such thing as a mistake-free parent. As a Dad, you will make mistakes, and you will make big mistakes, but if you love your children passionately, they will forgive you for those mistakes. Let your passion for loving others be known. Talk to your kids about love and about how much you love them. Tell them you love them. Show them your love. The saddest thing that ever happens is when our children have questions about our love. A Father who does not love and does not love well is a father who is failing his children. I know the last statement was harsh, but it is true. I have had over a hundred teenagers on probation and in the foster care system live in my house; the common denominator was either an absent father or a father who did not show them love. Dads, we are not perfect, so don't expect to be perfect. Just love your kids.

As I have already stated, I have been a father to many. I have had well over 100 teenagers live in my home. I have five children of my own. I have also had another 30 to 35 college-age students who, at one time or another, lived in my house and looked to me as a father. I led a discipleship school with hundreds of students looking to me for guidance. I was very much a father figure to many of those students. I am restating these things because I want you to understand that I get it. I know the challenges of being a father. I have had both victories and failures as a father. I hope that something in this book connects with you.

I was a foster parent for 11 years. I was named foster parent of the year on two separate occasions. I was given the Lieutenant Governor Award for my work with troubled teens. I have adopted one child and fathered two biological children, and by marrying my amazing wife, Elisabeth, I have two more children to whom I have been able to be a father. I have been a father of some kind for the last thirty-one years. I know how to be a dad, but hearing from some of those who lived in my home may be helpful.

Here are a few kids in my home who, now adults, reflect on our days together.

From Moriah (Biological Daughter)

I am proud of my dad. A big reason I am proud of him is because he is constantly changing. When my mom died, he had to become more soft-spoken and kind-hearted because those were the qualities that my mom had brought to me and my brother. As I've grown, I look back at our memories and noticed how much he's changed, and this is why he is truly an incredible dad.

One example of this is sitting at dinner with him and getting so angry at something he said because I thought it was mean. I looked at him and said, "that isn't love." Acting with love is important to me and it's important to him. He's always said "if you were going to get anything out of the Bible, let it be learning how to love people right." I remember him coming back to me later and admitting that I was right, which doesn't happen very often. I noticed him change his mind about things that didn't correlate with love. I'm not sure if he even truly realizes how much he's constantly changed to be better. He provided the love and patience a mom normally brings to the table. When I was younger he did my hair until I could do it myself. I am proud to say my dad is my best friend. He is the best dad in the world.

From May

I became a ward of the court when I was 15. I was a rebellious teenager who didn't follow her parents' rules: no sex, drugs, or rock and roll. I had my fair share of foster homes that fostered environments for bad behavior, choices, and lack of guidance. I had one foster mother who made me clean her kitchen floor with a toothbrush. One home encouraged a relationship with an older man, resulting in teenage pregnancy. When I turned 16, I again found myself in the juvenile hall, battling addiction, abandonment, depression, and guilt from the recent abortion.

I was given another chance and placed in the home of Willy and Martha Bowles. Something was greatly different in their home. There was a presence. One I had never felt before —one of love and encouragement, a feeling that encompassed my whole being and comforted my soul.

Willy and Martha, through love, taught me to forgive, receive love, accept punishment, experience forgiveness, and learn about the Lord. Martha taught me in the ways a natural mother would. A kind heart, a gentle word, and an open ear and heart. Willy taught me that there could be proper parenting done in a consistent fashion centered around Christ. Willy told me no many times but gave reasons and explanations for his decision. Not that I deserved an answer, but he wanted to teach me why. Willy took me around on his riding lawn mower as we joked about having a yard service, calling ourselves Willy Mays! Martha and I hid in the dark on a rainy night, waiting for Willy to come home. Once he stepped out of his car, we pelted him with marshmallows.... our laughs and squeals could be heard throughout the neighborhood— what a great memory. Willy, honoring the word of God, was the head of a household that he and Martha created for the troubled youth of the area. The home was filled with laughter, practical jokes, good food, prayer, devotion, and constant teaching. Willy and Martha introduced me to Christ. Beyond foster parents, Willy and Martha were Soul Winners. Today, Willy is still sold out to Christ and sold out to make a difference in the lives of Humboldt County.
I love you, Willy.

From Lilly

I entered Willy and Martha Bowles' home at the age of 16. Coming from a dysfunctional and abusive situation, I felt small, insignificant, unlovable, and alone. Other than a few of my siblings, there was nobody I really could rely on and trust. The Bowles became the parents of my heart. I stayed in the home until I was 19. After three years, I was shown more love and acceptance than in the 16 years prior. Many times, I pushed the limits to see just how far they were willing to go before giving up on me. Time and time again, I was shown unconditional love.

Willy and Martha were by my side, cheering me on as I moved forward and became the woman I am today. We had our ups and downs, but I learned what real love is all about. It dramatically changed the course my life was on.

When I was young, I learned that when a couple argued, it always led to violence and someone either getting arrested or not coming back. So, when Willy (Dad) and Martha (Mom) got into an argument in front of me for the first time, I was devastated. I remember listening with dread in my heart. In reality, it was just a fight. I think Mom's feelings were hurt by something Dad said. She was crying, and Dad walked out the door, got in the car, and left. I started to cry because I was sure it meant that he was not coming back. But Mom assured me everything was okay and he would return when they both had time to cool down. That they just needed their own space. Of course, she was right. He returned a little while later, and they calmly worked it out. They never fought behind closed doors. I think it was to show us that there was nothing to hide and that it didn't involve violence. They would never intentionally hurt each other. They said that they never went to bed angry. They always worked out their differences no matter how long it took. Watching them interact with each other and their love and respect for one another gave me an idea of what I wanted someday when I got married. Not all relationships are dysfunctional. One day, my parents, sister, and I were all in the car. We stopped by the church, where they were youth pastors, so my sister and I went to the store right down the street. Usually, we are at the church for long periods, so we just assumed it was all right. When we got done at the store, my parents were waiting for us, and Dad was upset. He started yelling about how he didn't have time to wait for us. I yelled back how we always waited for them, which made him mad. He said that when we got home, I could pack my things. Having been abandoned by most people in my life, I just knew that this day would come. No one ever stayed in my life for long. Lorraine was crying and asking me why I had to say that. I just kept my silence. I felt like I was dying inside. When we got home, I went to my room, and with tears streaming down my face, I neatly packed my things. I could hear my Mom and Dad talking heatedly downstairs. After a few minutes, they came into my room to talk to me. Mom asked me what I was doing, and I told her I was packing my things. She told me to stop, and when I didn't, she gently placed her hand on mine. She explained that tension was high because of her health issues and that she and Dad were under a lot of stress. I said that they were not the only ones worried about her. It affected all of us. Dad said that I was right, that he was sorry, and that I wasn't going anywhere. I said that I was sorry, and we all hugged it out.

From Nate

Willy taught me how to be a man. I am a good father today because of the lessons I learned in his house. Mostly I just watched what he did. Willy and Martha loved me like no one else had ever loved me. I came to their house when I was 12 years old and left the house when I was 17. It was the first time I was ever cared for and loved. They showed me that there was a different life than the one I had experienced before that. They showed me that I could be something different than I had been taught to be at that point in my life. Willy was my Foster Dad, youth pastor, and High School Football Coach. I remember having to run and do my homework at the same time. He pushed me to be more than I ever thought I could be. I learned what was important in life from Willy. I remember the time when bears would come to the house, and Willy would chase them off, and then one night, we actually had a skunk in the house. That was a time I will never forget. Acceptance was the key to living with Willy and Martha. We were not their kids, but they accepted us like we were. My favorite event was when we all went to Yosemite. In the middle of the night, something turned over our tent; we were screaming for Willy, and sure enough, he came running. Willy taught me that you have to love yourself before you can love anybody else. When I went to Willy's house, I was told that I would never be allowed to go back to a city school. I was too bad of a kid to be let into a city school. When I went to Willy and Martha's house, it was only three months or so, and they had me back into a regular city school where I began to thrive. Today, my children are a product of the lessons I learned from Willy. Because of Willy and Martha, I broke the chain of dysfunction in my family. Willy is the only person I know who will always answer the phone. He has always answered, and I know to this day that he always will answer. I love you, pop!

Why we need fathers today more than ever

"Because of Willy and Martha, I broke the chain of dysfunction in my family." - Nate

If you know anything about foster parents, you'll know it's never stable. Some kids were there for only a few days, some for a few years, but most were there for a few months. We took the teenagers that nobody else wanted. Most of the teens we took into our home were on probation and considered "bad kids." We took both boys and girls, and our first contact with them was almost always when we would go into Juvenile Hall and meet them. Here is what we found most of the time during that first meeting. The teen usually had no functioning parent at home. The parent or parental figure at home was almost always addicted to drugs and/or alcohol; most of the time, the absent parent was the father. On many occasions, the teens had never met their father because he was either completely absent, unknown, or incarcerated. The mom, grandmother, aunt, or other parental figure was on welfare, and drugs were often prevalent at home. We also found that on many occasions, the kids in our home had parents who had also been a part of the foster care system when they were children. One family could never think back to a time in their family history when there were two parents in the home. For some of the families, this was an epidemic of generations. They were in foster care; their parents had been in foster care, and if the foster care system had existed during their grandparents' time, they would have been in foster care. Children in these homes grow up with disadvantages that few can comprehend. What does it mean for children to grow up in homes without fathers? In today's world, political correctness says that any parent will do. Mom or Dad, it doesn't matter. A parent is a parent, but political correctness brings a horrible reality to our world. Boys need their Dads, and girls need their Daddies.

To demonstrate this point, let me present a paper on the damaging effects of not having a father, as seen in the *Elephants of Kruger National Park and Game Reserve in South Africa*, as told by 60 Minutes.

(*August 22, 2000 Sixty Minutes* CBS.) The park was faced with a growing elephant problem. Once an endangered species, the population of African elephants had grown more extensive than the park could sustain. Measures had to be taken to thin the ranks. A plan was devised to relocate some of the elephants to other African game reserves. Elephants cannot be transported very easily because they are just too large. A special harness was created to air-lift the elephants and fly them out of the park using helicopters. The helicopters and harnesses were up to the task when it came to the juvenile and female elephants, but harnesses could not hold the giant African bull elephants. A quick solution had to be found, so a decision was made to leave the much larger bulls at Kruger and relocate only some of the female elephants and juvenile males.

The problem was solved. The herd was thinned out, and all was well at Kruger National Park. Sometime later, however, a strange problem surfaced at South Africa's other game reserve, Pilanesburg National Park, the younger elephants' new home. Rangers at Pilanesburg began finding the dead bodies of endangered white rhinoceros. At first, it was thought maybe poachers had killed the White rhinos, but they had not died of gunshot wounds, and their precious horns were left intact. The rhinos appeared to be killed violently, with deep puncture wounds. Not much in the wild can kill a rhino, so rangers set up hidden cameras throughout the park. The result was shocking. The culprits turned out to be marauding bands of aggressive juvenile male elephants. The very elephants relocated from Kruger National Park a few years earlier. The young males were caught on camera chasing down the rhinos, knocking them over, stomping, and goring them to death with their tusks. The juvenile elephants were terrorizing other animals in the park as well. Such behavior was rare, very rare among elephants. Something had gone wrong.

Some of the park rangers settled on a theory. The presence of large dominant bulls that remained at Kruger had been missing from the relocated herd. In natural circumstances, the adult bulls provide modeling behaviors for younger elephants, keeping them in line. Wade Horn, Ph.D., President of the National Fatherhood Initiative, pointed out that juvenile male elephants experience "musth," a state of frenzy triggered by mating season and increases in testosterone. Typically, dominant bulls manage and contain testosterone-induced rage in younger males. They do this by role-modeling what an adult elephant does, much like a father with a teenage boy would do. Left without elephant modeling, the rangers theorized that the younger elephants were missing the civilizing influence of their elders as nature and pachyderm protocol intended. To test the theory, the rangers constructed a bigger and stronger harness, then flew in some of the older bulls left behind at Kruger. Within weeks, the bizarre and violent behavior of the juvenile elephants stopped completely. The example set by the older bulls provided a model for the juveniles of the elephant-like behavior. In a short time, the younger elephants followed the older and more dominant bulls while learning how to be elephants.

Daniel Patrick Moynihan wrote some forty years ago," From the wild Irish slums of the 19th Century Eastern Seaboard to the riot-torn suburbs of Los Angeles, there is one unmistakable lesson in American history: A community that allows a large number of young men to grow up in broken homes led primarily by women, never acquiring any stable relationship to male authority, never acquiring any rational expectations for the future – that community asks for and gets chaos."

A society without fathers is a doomed society. Young men need fathers. They need them as role models and guideposts, and they need them as examples. When I was growing up, there were certain lines I didn't cross because I knew if I did, I would have to face my father. Fathers, you must be kind, loving role models who can also tell your son, "You will not act like that again." I remember one occasion when my dad made this point clear to me. One day, when I was twelve, I had a moment of confrontation with my mother. My mom was great at being a mother, but I was a boy of twelve trying to understand my place in the world. That day, my father, for some reason, was home from work during a time when I was positive he was at work. Unknown to me, he was sitting in the living room, and I was coming into the house through our garage. Coming in from the garage, I had to go into the kitchen and walk through the kitchen before I could see into the living room. That day, I decided to call my mother a bitch when she asked me to do something. Now, no day is a good day to call your mother a bitch, but that day, as my father was sitting in the living room hearing everything that took place, was definitely not the right day. As I called my mom a bitch and turned the corner into our living room, I ran straight into my dad, who made it crystal clear that I would NEVER do something like that again. On that day, I was a marauding twelve-year-old who needed to understand what men do and do not do. Thank God I had a father who taught me this lesson. That was a mistake I never repeated. Boys need grown men who can teach and show them what it means to be a man. The most dangerous thing on the planet is a group of boys who have no fathers or father figures and are left to themselves to explore what life looks like. Without restraint, adolescent boys will do almost anything if they have a friend or two who will go along with them. I think back to my early years and realize the thought of what my dad would do to me if I did "that thing" kept me out of a lot of trouble. Sometimes, the thought of what Dad will think or do is the most powerful thought of all, especially if Dad is engaged. But let's face it, it's not just about acting right; it is also about safety. Boys do dumb things. When I was a child, I had a group of friends, and we used to go out into a field by our homes and shoot an arrow straight up into the sky to see who would stand there the longest as the arrow fell back to the ground. These same friends used to lie down in the middle of a busy street to see who would stay there the longest as cars approached. Boys do dumb things. Dr. James Dobson once summed up the difference between boys and girls like this, if a girl jumps off a fence and hurts herself, she will instinctively say that it is a bad idea and never jump off a fence or anything else again. If a boy jumps off the same fence and hurts himself, he will instinctively want to do it again to try to figure out how to do it without getting hurt. Boys and girls are different. Boys need guidance in almost every area of life. When my mother told me to stop shooting arrows in the air because someone would get hurt, I would ignore her. Why? Because she had never done this before and didn't understand how fun it was. Besides, she was my mom and not really a threat. When my dad said, "Son, if you do that again, I will beat your butt until it is raw", I understood that I could no longer do that without severe consequences. (I am not endorsing spanking, but this is a true story). Boys need a structure that says you cannot do that; if you do, there will be consequences. Boys need a father.

A skunk in the house

"I remember the time when bears would come to the house, and Willy would chase them off, and then one night, we actually had a skunk in the house." - Nate

It was 2:00 in the morning. My wife and I had been asleep for several hours, and the phone rang. Now, I don't know about your house, but at my house, when the phone rings in the early morning hours, it usually means only one thing. Something terrible has happened this early morning. My wife and I had six teenagers, all on probation and all foster kids living in our home. We also had a nanny living with us. In total, nine of us lived in a seventeen-hundred-square-foot home. The house we lived in was an old barn we'd bought and were remodeling. At the time, the only way to get upstairs was to go outside and use the exterior stairs at the back of the house. Upstairs lived our four teenage boys and our nanny. Downstairs were our two teenage girls, my wife and myself. The old barn, now a house, was located in the woods. The boys, being typical teenagers, had several bad habits. First, even though they were asked over and over again not to take food upstairs, all of them did. Second, I had asked them over and over again to make sure the door they used upstairs was closed because being in the woods meant a backyard full of forest creatures. I had seen mountain lions, bears, raccoons, skunks, and many other animals right out our back door. Keeping the doors closed was a good idea unless they wanted unwelcome visitors.

This morning, our phone rang, and in a groggy haze, my mind began preparing itself for whatever tragedy was on the other end. After all, I am a pastor, and these early morning phone calls are not usually good news. "Hello," I said, "Will." It was one of the boys from upstairs. "Yes," I said, wondering what could be an emergency coming from upstairs, "I think there is a skunk under my bed." "Say that again," I blurted out. "I think there is a skunk under my bed." By now, my wife was awake and extremely curious as to what the commotion could be. I turned to her and said, "Jimmy says he has a skunk in his room under his bed." My immediate thought was that it had to be a cat. I'm sure it's a cat. Skunks don't live in houses, but cats do. So, I assured my wife that it was probably a cat and no big deal. I told her to go back to sleep while I went to get the cat out of the room.

Upstairs, I found all the boys outside on the deck waiting for me to take care of this skunk. I assured them it was a cat and tried to get them to go back to bed. They were not going back to bed. None of them were going back to bed. Even our nanny was up then and was not going back to bed either. Okay, I thought, let's get this over with. I proceeded to the back bedroom where the "skunk" was supposed to be. When I arrived, Jimmy pointed to the bed and said, "Look at the back corner." I pointed my flashlight in the corner under the bed and saw not a cat or even some delicate white-stripped skunk but a huge evil monster of a skunk. None of the foster parenting classes I'd ever taken offered a session on skunk removal.

Some of you may be asking why I didn't call an exterminator. Some of us have to learn from our mistakes, and that night with the skunk was my turn to be educated. After seeing that it was a skunk and not the cat I'd been hoping for, I evacuated upstairs. The nanny, the boys, and myself all headed for the first floor of our home. If we left it alone, I felt like it would return home to the woods where skunks should be. So we all went downstairs and waited for the skunk to leave. We waited and waited, and waited, for two hours. By 4:00 am, I thought the skunk would have left, so I went back upstairs. Nope, the skunk was still there. Two hours being plenty of time, I decided it was time to take action, and I had come up with the perfect plan. I had decided to coax the skunk outside using a long pole. In my shed, I had a piece of plastic pipe that was about ten feet in length. I figured I could very gently start prodding the skunk outside. I knew that as I did this, there was a chance that the skunk might spray, so I had all the boys move everything out of the skunk's intended exit path. We moved everything except the bed the skunk was under and a dresser with a TV in the corner. The TV, one of those 32-inch console TVs from 1994, was too heavy to lift. Once the room was ready with everything that could be moved out of the way, I began to coax the skunk. Armed with my ten-foot-long pole, I gently push him toward the bedroom door.

I'm coaxing the skunk. The skunk and I are slowly moving across the bedroom. My plan is working! We get to the hallway, and everything is going as planned. The skunk is almost there. Ten more feet is the exterior door. When we get to the hall, the skunk takes off, running straight for the exit. I have done it!" I started thinking to myself, "I should be called a skunk whisperer. Maybe I have just fallen into a new career. Who needs exterminators when you have Willy the Skunk Whisperer? I have done it! I have conquered the skunk." What? The skunk has stopped. He is looking right at me. After a brief stare-down, the skunk starts running straight for me. The monster is running straight for me, "No," I scream and jump back into the dresser holding the TV. The TV crashes to the ground. The huge, monstrous, fanged, bigger than anything I have ever seen skunk runs back under the bed. This time, it crawls into the box spring, not just under the bed. No more coaxing, the skunk had dug himself in, and he was not coming out.

In case you're visualizing this as you read, let me assure you how well I handled that situation. I never lost my temper. I never uttered anything I should not have, no curse words, no frustration. I was a perfect angel throughout this entire event. If you believe that I have some beachfront property in Nebraska, I would like to sell it to you.

I reacted as you would expect someone to react upon finding a skunk in their house at 2:00 am. I was a wreck; it was now 4:30, we had barely slept, and we were dealing with a disaster. And there was still a skunk in the house.

More drastic measures now had to be taken. Jimmy and I decided to go into the room, pull the mattress off the bed, grab the box spring where the skunk had become fully entrenched, flip the box on its side to fit in the hallway, run it outside, and throw it off the deck. You might have an opinion on the quality of this plan, but I was hopeful. So, Jimmy and I went into the room and executed the plan flawlessly.

Unfortunately, the skunk was not a willing participant in our plan. As soon as we picked up the box spring, the skunk did what skunks do and started spraying. By the time we reached the deck and tossed the box spring, Jimmy, myself, and the entire upstairs was now engulfed in a fog of skunk spray. The skunk, having decided the box spring was home, no matter where it landed, stayed where he was. I was mad, upset, furious, bewildered, and had a hundred other negative emotions flooding me all at once. I was not in my right mind, and I decided revenge was now my next move. I went to my shed for some gasoline and poured it everywhere, intending to light the skunk on fire.

I am not a mind reader, but I bet you think that is horrible for me to have done. You are right! It was horrible. All I can say is it was 4:30 in the morning, and my thought process was not functioning correctly. I poured the gas on the box spring, lit the match, and I had a fire. A lot of fire. What a minute! That is too much fire. Oh my God, I have to get a hose! For the animal lovers, relax. The skunk was not affected by this in any way. It calmly exited the box spring and ran off into the woods, where I assume he lived happily ever after. He even winked at me as he left. Okay, maybe he didn't do that, but it sure felt like that as he walked off into the woods.

Unfortunately, I now had a large fire in my backyard, which left me sprinting for a garden hose. About 30 minutes later, I got the fire out. It was now around 5:00 am, and we all just needed to get some sleep. I decided to send the boys upstairs to get their pillows and bedding so they could sleep downstairs. The skunk smell was everywhere. We could tackle the cleanup tomorrow.

Since I consider myself a good father, I'm always looking for learning lessons. As I've said, we live in the woods, and I repeatedly told the boys to shut the back door. I had explained to them many times that wild animals live in the woods and would love to come into the nice, warm house. This seemed like the perfect teachable moment after what we had just been through.

Before I sent them to get their things, I reminded the boys that this is why we don't leave the doors open. I reminded them about the wild animals. I pointed to the backyard, now scorched by fire. This, this right here, is what I have been talking about.

With those parting thoughts, I sent them to get their things. A few minutes later, after they'd all made beds on the floor, I was lying down, tired but kind of satisfied because I had just turned a disaster into a teachable moment. As I was lying there congratulating myself on this great lesson they have undoubtedly learned, a thought went through my mind, "They just went upstairs to get their stuff. Is there any chance they left the back door open?". "No way," I thought. There was no chance they left the back door open, especially after all that had happened. Just to be sure, I better check. So, I got up confidently and went outside, knowing I would see the back door closed.

As soon as I walked out, I looked up the stairs, and can you believe the back door was wide open? It was not a good night. I lost my last remaining grasp on calm, and the boys knew I was done.

Sometimes, fathering is a lot like finding a skunk in the house. It can be a disaster. All fathers fail. All parents fail. I have failed as a father, and so will you. Let's face it: sometimes, I am the skunk in the house. Sometimes, my attitude is more offensive than any skunk I have ever come across. When you fail, learn to say you are sorry and mean it. Failure cannot be the focus, and you cannot let failure define who you are. You have to learn to work through whatever tragedy is before you and know that life will get better.

The skunk being in our house, as bad as it was, does not in any way define my time with those kids in our house. Those boys would have rather lived in that house with a skunk than not be in that home at all. They found a place, a father, a mother, and a family that loved them, and living with a skunk was not the focus.

Maybe you are not even a father and just accidentally stumbled on this book. I don't know what is happening with you right now. I don't know what tragedy is before you or what you have to go through, but I can tell you it will get better. The skunk will leave your house, and you can move forward.

Yes, there will be cleanup involved. We had to strip the carpeting, the padding, and the texture from the walls and completely redo the upstairs area to get the smell of the skunk out of our house. It was a major pain to clean up, but we got it done. You will conquer whatever is before you. You have got this! How do I know you have got this? Because I am proof. In my life, I have faced tragedies and made mistakes. I have made plenty of mistakes, but I have kept moving forward. Failure only exists when we stop trying. I don't know where you are when it comes to faith, but I believe in a God of endless chances. You might have made mistakes, but you can still change. Even if your kids are adults, change now. You can do this! The only real mistake is when we stop trying. Keep pushing forward. It is never too late.

Let's Go Fishing

"I was given another chance and placed in the home of Willy and Martha Bowles. Something was greatly different in their home. There was a presence. One I had never felt before—one of love and encouragement, a feeling that encompassed my whole being and comforted my soul." - May

One night around 9:00 PM, early in my foster parenting tenure, I told the four boys who lived with us that we were "gonna go fishing." It wasn't a big deal. A little pier a few miles away from our home stretched out over the bay. It was a lovely night, and I had plenty of time. I had some fishing poles and knew of a store where we could buy bait even though it was late. So I grabbed the boys, and we headed out. One of the boys with us, Bobby, had only been in our home for a few weeks. Bobby was a good kid but had gotten in trouble and was now on probation. He was a tough kid but also a very sweet, tender-hearted kid who had just had a bad situation at home. Walking out to the pier, I noticed that Bobby had fallen behind. I knew the other boys were heading in the right direction, and I could see the dock from where we were, so I stopped and waited for him. As Bobby grew closer, I realized he had tears in his eyes. He was crying. I had no idea why he was crying, so I began to ask a few simple questions. I'll never forget what he told me that night when I asked him what was wrong.

"My dad promised to take me fishing my whole life, and never once did he ever keep his promise. I have lived in your house for two weeks, and you are already taking me fishing". Dads, keep the promises you make to your children. Bobby's dad was an alcoholic and often made promises he could not or would not keep. His entire life, Bobby had promises made to him that were never kept. He had promised to go fishing and camping, promises that his dad would attend a special event at school, but they were all broken. I can only imagine what he thought when he heard me announce we would go fishing. "Oh great, here we go again, another guy making a promise that isn't going to happen." His Dad had made promises he did not keep throughout his life. What kind of an example was his dad for him? As a child growing up, the model was that if his dad said it, it wouldn't happen. Bobby was in tears that night for many reasons, but that was the first time a father had ever kept his word to him.

I learned a valuable lesson that night. When you say you will do something, you better do it. Bobby had a great night of fishing, we all did. None of us caught a fish; I don't think we even got a bite. In fact, of the many times I took the boys in our home on those fishing trips, I cannot ever remember catching a single fish, but it was never about fishing. It was about spending time and being a man of my word. Fathers can make a lot of mistakes. Mistakes are part of life. But the biggest mistake I see fathers make is when they are not men of their word. A promise to a child is not just a promise. It is something more than that. A promise to a child represents faith. Children believe us when we tell them something. I think that is what Jesus was talking about, or at least one of the things He was talking about, when he said, "Unless you become like one of these children, you will not see the Kingdom of God." Matthew 18:3. Children have incredible faith! But when fathers do not keep their word, they teach their children that faith cannot be trusted. Dad, be a man of your word.

Now, let's get real for a moment. No father will ever keep his word 100% of the time. After all, life happens, and part of that is teaching our children to be flexible, but if keeping your word seems harder and harder to do, then you need to do something differently. Yes, there will be times when you have planned a day to go fishing, and you can't make that trip for whatever reason. It's okay! Apologize and move on, but that cannot become a habit.

I want to be clear here and talk about Bobby's dad. Please understand that I am not picking on his dad. I am sure there are many reasons his dad was the way he was. Bobby's dad had probably had the same example in life. One of the things I found doing foster care is that many parents who had lost their kids to the foster care system had themselves been in that system. I would not be surprised if Bobby's father had been raised in the house of an alcoholic. Perhaps you were raised in a dysfunctional home. I heard someone say once that you are not responsible for what happened to you as a child, but as an adult, you are 100% responsible for how you deal with what happened to you as a child. Dad, if this is you, it is time to start taking care of your own issues so you can be a better dad. Your children need you, and our world needs you. You can do this; you can make a change.

My father came from a very dysfunctional home. My grandfather was a World War II hero. He was a great soldier. He was bigger than life, but unfortunately, my grandfather was a better soldier than a father. My grandfather would often put the family in the car and move from one place to another. He was always looking for the greener grass on the other side of the fence, but unfortunately, he never found that place. So, they moved, and they moved and then moved again. This took a tremendous toll on my dad, uncles, and aunt.

Drinking, drugs, and sex were all part of their childhood experiences. In fact, on my side of the family, a family reunion was never an option. I have had uncles who were alcoholics and an aunt who has been in prison for several different reasons. They have all had issues that they needed to conquer. I am happy to report that they are all in a much better place. They have done the hard work to change, and they have broken the cycle of disfunction. When my dad and mom got married, my dad was the wild child, and my mom was the daughter of an Assembly of God pastor. She was not only a conservative, she was on the far, far, farther, keep going right version of conservatives. It didn't take long before those two worlds conflicted. When I was about two, my dad decided to change his life, and here is how that decision came about. One night, my dad was out partying and got pretty drunk. When it was time for him to go home, his buddies would not let him drive drunk, so they brought him home.

They drove to the house, put him on the front lawn, honked the horn, and took off. My father was so drunk he could barely stand, and rumor has it he was missing a few articles of clothing. My mom and dad fought that night right there on the front lawn. While they were fighting, I woke up and went to see what was happening. Much later in life, my dad described what happened to him at that moment. He said, "When I saw you, the thought went through my head: my son will not grow up like me." Right then and there, my dad changed his life. My dad was not responsible for what happened to him as a child, but as an adult, he was 100% responsible for how he handled what happened to him. Because of that, I grew up in a home much different than the one my father did. I grew up in a house where I never remember my father drinking or having alcohol until my sister and I were adults. This, by the way, is not an indictment on alcohol. If you are twenty-one, do not have addiction tendencies, and drink responsibly, that is your choice. I am just telling my story. I am who I am today because I had a father who was determined to break the chain of dysfunction in his life.

I grew up different than my dad. As a kid, we moved four times, and one of those was only a few blocks away to a bigger house. I had stability, which was something my dad never had. My dad took responsibility as an adult for what happened to him as a child and became the most incredible man I have ever known.

Dads, parents, you can break the chain of dysfunction and start a life of stability and freedom for your children. The generations that follow will benefit from this for years to come. My kids have benefited, and their kids will benefit because of the decisions my dad made. Break the cycle of dysfunction. It is never too late to do so, but the earlier you break it off, the more benefit those around you will get.

Parenting fails, and I'm sorry.

"Dad said that I was right, that he was sorry, and that I wasn't going anywhere. I said that I was sorry, and we all hugged it out."-Lilly

When my son Will was three or four years old, he loved video games. They were by far his favorite thing to do. At that time, we had three foster sons who had been with us since before Will was born. My wife and I had planned on being out of foster care before we had our own children for many reasons, but one of those reasons was that we often had teens in our home who had been abused sexually as children.

One of the things you may or may not be aware of is that children who are abused sexually sometimes abuse others in the same way. We never wanted to run that kind of risk with our children. That is one of the reasons we only took teenagers and not younger children into our home. We wanted the kids to be close to the same ages. Since we started with a teen girl who was in our youth group, teens are what we stayed with.

At the time, the boys we had in the home were ones we trusted, but in the words of one of our former President's Ronald Regan, "trust but verify." I decided that I needed to make sure Will knew and understood how to come to me and tell me if anything inappropriate happened. I decided to tell Will that if anybody ever touched his penis and he told me about it, I'd buy him a new video game. I now know that was the wrong thing to say to a three-year-old, but it seemed like a reasonable solution at the time. One day, the three of us, my wife Martha, Will and myself, were in the car, Will was in the back seat. Out of the back, I hear his voice say, "Dad, do you remember when you said if anyone touches my penis, I will get a new video game?" Instantly terrified, I gripped the steering wheel of our Nissan mini-van, and my knuckles began to turn white. I looked at my wife and calmly pulled over to the side of the road. My brain running through all of the worst possible scenarios. My voice cracked as I replied, "Yes, son, has someone touched your penis?" With all the anticipation of Christmas morning, I heard his little voice reply from behind me, "Not yet!" The hopeful yet innocent air of anticipation sent us on a laughter spree that lasted for several minutes. Laughing, at least, until his mom began to process what I had said and started to question my sanity. I still remember her looking at me and asking, "Why would you ever say that to a three-year-old?"

What is the point of this story? Even with the best intentions, we can do things completely wrong. I had to say I was sorry to my three-year-old son and my wife that day. We all make mistakes. What mistakes have you made?

"I'm sorry." Those two words may be the most important words your children ever hear you say. Dad, you're not perfect. Your kids know you are not perfect, so stop pretending to be perfect. There have been many times in raising my kids where I have just been flat wrong. Let's face it: nobody is perfect, and everybody makes mistakes. Men, we don't like to be wrong. We feel like being wrong is a sign of weakness, and if you are like me, you don't like looking weak. But if you are like me, you are also not sure what you feel most of the time. Most men are not good at feelings. I know it's another stereotype, but in my experience, it is true.

I once had a therapist who told me that our emotions could be grouped into four categories. Mad, sad, glad, or scared. I was going to therapy with my wife because we had marriage problems. We had only been married for a year, and we were in deep trouble. Honestly, I didn't think we would be married much longer, and my wife fully agreed with my assessment. I am pretty sure neither one of us even wanted to continue our marriage, but because we were in ministry, youth pastors at a church, simply giving up was not an option. Divorce at that time would have meant we both would have lost our job, so we had agreed to enter therapy. During therapy, our therapist made us sit in a chair face to face and play a game called mad, sad, glad, scared. As we sat there staring at each other, we had to go through each emotion and say everything we felt. For instance, if I started, I would start by saying I am mad about this… and I would continue until I had run out of all the things I was mad about. Then, when I was done, my wife would go.

We did this for each emotion: mad, sad, glad, scared. My list of things I was mad at was always long, I mean really long. So it seemed the time it took to go through everything I was mad at always took forever. After I was done with my mads, my wife would go, and it was her turn to say all of her mad things. Usually, her list of mad things consisted of one or two things. As we moved through the list, it was easy to see one of the ways that we were opposite. After mad, the next emotion was sad. I would have maybe two or three of these, but my wife would have a list longer than my arm. That was about the way it went for the rest of the game. Glad was always both of us trying to pick out something that we were glad about, even though we had just spilled our guts about the rest of our feelings.

I was mad, or at least I thought I was mad, and she was everything else. Why is that? I believe it's because, as men, we feel vulnerable if we are sad or scared. If I admit I am sad or scared, I feel like I am not a good or strong man. Men, think about that for a minute. Is that true? We have projected such an image of what a man is supposed to be that now we allow that image to control us. That is the whole point of the Marlboro Man.

What is being manly? I am a man, so anything I choose to do should be manly. I like flowers. I want to have flowers in my house and like to have flowers in the yard. Does that make me less manly? I don't think so. We have created an image of manhood that is not sustainable. I do not like working on cars, engines, or anything related to those fields. I will not even change my oil. Why? Because I don't like it. Does that make me less of a man? If a woman wants to do those things, does that make her less of a woman? Of course not. Can we stop putting all of these false social constraints around each other? Don't you think this could be part of the problem we see today around the issues of gender?

Can we just leave people alone and let them do what makes them happy? Years ago, women could not be doctors, lawyers, or politicians, and it was frowned upon if men became nurses, teachers, and stay-at-home dads. But does any of that matter? Does it make them less of a man or woman because they do not follow traditional roles? I have a female doctor. Thank God for her. My children have had amazing men as teachers, and I thank God for them. When my first wife was in the hospital on several occasions, she had male nurses. They were terrific examples of what a man should be. I thanked God for each one of them.

It is not about what you do but about who you are. Are you a good person? Are you generous and kind? Have you brought love into the lives of your kids? Have you gotten in touch with your feelings so you can be an effective dad? We, as men, should be in touch with our feelings and in touch with who we are. I should have, you should have, more emotions than just being pissed off all the time. When I say things like I am sad or scared, that should not be a point to question my manhood. Men get some emotions. Let people in. Your kids need to see you with a range of emotions: sad, glad, and scared. If they see you with a range of emotions, they also have permission to explore their emotions.

When they hear you say I am sorry, they know that is a standard for them. Start setting a standard that lets your kids know that their emotions are important and they are accountable for those emotions. A father who never apologizes is a father who is setting his kids up for failure. Dad, say you are sorry, and back it up with change.

It's a Dance!

"When I turned 16, I again found myself in the juvenile hall, battling addiction, abandonment, depression, and guilt from the recent abortion." - May

I once asked a friend of mine what the secret to parenting was. He is a great father and a good friend, and I value his opinion. I found his response interesting. "Every child is a new dance," he said, "How you parent one child will not be how you parent another." I understood that, but I had never thought to put it that way. I now realize that the dance may even change in the middle of the song. Your child will need different things depending on what is going on with them right now. While doing foster care, we were parenting teens who had all grown up in different homes and had different experiences, so they were all totally different. But how does that happen when you have siblings who grow up in the same house, under the same circumstances, with virtually no differences?

My children, who have grown up in the same house, are as different as night is from the day. One of my sons is an introvert. He values the time he has alone. He is 24 and lives alone in his apartment. He loves it! One of my daughters is an extreme extrovert. The more people around her, the better. I cannot imagine her ever wanting to live alone.

One of my daughters is a rule follower, another one believes rules are more of a suggestion or even an afterthought. One of my daughters has a very dialed-in room. Everything has a place. Her shoes are lined up in a certain way, and her clothes are all facing the same way in her closet, and all of her hangers are the same color. Another one of my other daughters last saw the carpet in her bedroom a couple of years ago because that is where her clothes go. Her shoes are not lined up, and her clothes stay on the floor. Each child is a unique dance because each child has a distinct personality, which is okay. That is one of the great things about humanity. All of us are different, each with our own personality. We see life differently.

Fathers must understand that what works for one child will not work for another. What is essential for one child is not necessary for the other. With my extroverted daughter, grounding her or limiting her interaction with friends is by far the worst punishment that could ever happen to her. With my other daughter, grounding her or telling her she cannot hang out with friends is like a reward. She didn't want to go anywhere to begin with.

As a father, I am responsible for discovering what my kids are into, what they like, and what they value. If you find out what they value, then you get a peek into their heart. My daughter, whose carpet you cannot find, is one of the most creative people ever. Walking into her room is like walking into a living collage. She has stuff on every part of her wall: posters, pictures, street signs, and more. It is a fantastic sight. It is messy but amazing. I don't know what career she will choose, but it will likely include being creative. How you deal with a creative person is different than how you would deal with someone else who is not.

Dad, what is your child into? What do they value? I have heard the scripture Proverbs 22:6 misquoted so many times I can hardly stand it. You know the one, "Start children off on the way they should go, and even when they are old, they will not turn from it." Many interpret that to mean to teach children how to be like you. That is WRONG. The scripture says to train up a child in the way THEY should go. Did you hear that? Not the way you think they should go. Dad, we must stop putting our expectations on our children and let them discover their own path. I played football in high school, and I played football in college. I also coached high school football for nineteen years. For most of my son's life, I was coaching football. The day he was born, I had a home game to coach that night, and I am embarrassed to say that I was on the sidelines. My son went to many practices as a child. He knows how important football was to me in my life. The year before my son started high school, I stopped coaching. I stopped for many reasons, but mainly because I didn't want my son to feel pressured to play or do something he did not want. If he went out for football, I wanted that to be his decision, not because of pressure from my life. So, I stopped coaching, and guess what? My son did not play football. He went out for cross-country but decided that wasn't for him. My son is not an athlete; he is athletic but just not interested in sports. He is a deep thinker, and he will accomplish things I could never do, even if I tried. I could not be more proud of him and who he is. My high school experience was very different than my son's experience, but my son did what he was supposed to do for who he is, and I am seeing him bloom now.

Each of our children is different, which is sometimes hard to navigate. When my son Will graduated from high school, I wanted to throw him a graduation party. I was planning and figuring out what to do. How big should the party be? Should we have dinner or just do finger foods? While pondering these questions, my wife asked me, "Does Will even want a party?"

"Of course he does. It's his graduation."

"How do you know that?" She asked.

"Because it is a graduation, and you have a party after graduation." I was very confident in my response.

"You better ask Will first."

So I did. Will did not want a party. It just wasn't something he was interested in. He just wanted to have a few friends around to celebrate. I was putting my expectations on my son. It is easy to do! I thought I was doing something he wanted, but it was only really what I wanted. Stop assuming you know what your children want and start asking them. One of my daughters, the extrovert, is getting ready to graduate in a few months. Does she want a party? She does and has already started making plans. Each child is a unique dance. Figure out their rhythm, and parenting will go a lot smoother.

As a coach, I cannot tell you how often I saw parents who had put their expectations on their sons. I had kids playing football who honestly hated playing football, but they played because they knew their fathers wanted them to play. It is such a bummer to see a child doing something because their parents want them to and not because they want to. I had one rule with my kids, which I learned from my parents. If you start something, you have to finish it. Before I go any further here, let me ensure we are all on the same page. I am talking about children making commitments and following through. I am not talking about keeping commitments in abusive situations. If my kids or anybody end up in an abusive situation, that is not something you finish. You run. Get out of the toxic, harmful environment as soon as you can. If you don't want to play a sport, don't play, but you will not stop something you have already started unless there is a valid reason. Abuse is always a reason to leave.

Not quitting was a lesson I learned from my mom. I already told you I played football in high school, but I only started playing as a junior. Unfortunately, the first week of practice is known as hell week. It is called hell week for obvious reasons. You go to practice, you start running, and you don't stop until the end of the week. For someone who is not in very good shape, it does represent hell. So I show up, and Hell Week starts. Two days later, I was in our living room telling my mom that I was going to quit the team. I hoped my mom would take time to pray about my decision and think about my feelings, but that wasn't the case. The moment I said I was going to quit, the words that came out of my extremely conservative mother were, "The hell you are. I already bought you cleats, and the season has already started." That was the end of the discussion. When my extremely conservative mom started cursing I knew the discussion was over. I had started and was going to finish; to this day, that was one of the best formative decisions my parents ever made. I cannot tell you the lessons I learned about teamwork and how my current career parallels many things I learned through playing and coaching football.

My parents didn't care if I played football or not. What they cared about was instilling in me the lessons of being a productive citizen. As parents, we must teach our children certain things that will help them in life. The former example is one of those things. Don't be a quitter just because it is hard. There are other lessons in life that we need to teach our children. Love, kindness, and caring are all part of those things. But what your child should become or what your child should do is up to them. As parents, we must be brave enough to get out of our children's way. Let their personalities shine even when they are opposite to ours. My wife, Elisabeth, has helped me work through some of these blind spots in my life. She has helped me learn that I tend to automatically think people think the same way I do. I even do this with our children. Remember the graduation party that I thought my son wanted to have? I felt he wanted a party because I would have liked that. People are different, and our children are different. Let's learn how to be dads who train our children up in the way THEY should go. If our kids discover who they are and we celebrate them for who they are, the world we live in will be much better.

Let's talk more about the dance. You may not have taken dance lessons, but I have. My first foray into dance was as a freshman in college. Our football coach decided that, as a team, we needed to get "lighter" on our feet. Imagine a dance class full of guys who didn't want to be there and were pretty bad at dancing; then, you can imagine how the class went. I remember feeling sorry for our instructor in the class. She tried hard, but I am afraid she was set up for failure. We did that dance class for an entire semester, and at the end of the class, not one of us was any better at dancing. That result is not far from my other experience with dance. My wife, Elisabeth, is an experienced dancer. She danced for many years. Then, one day, she tore her Achilles heel at a ballet class. After her injury, she decided she needed to do something else that wasn't as demanding on her Achilles, so now she is a boxer. Yes, you heard me right; her easier solution was to begin to take boxing lessons. What can I say? My wife is a badass.

Before her injury, I wanted to connect with her in her world. Which means I decided to take social dance lessons with my wife. She didn't need lessons, but it was something that we could do together, and I thought it would be fun learning something new. We took lessons for a few months. She was great, and I was, let's say I wasn't. I could not get my feet to move as they were supposed to. I tried, I did, but no matter what I did, I felt, looked, and was clumsy. Learning how to dance can be hard, really hard, but learning how to be a better father doesn't have to be.

Dad, you are going to fail. It is ok. Effort goes a long way when it comes to parenting. Have lots of conversations with your kids. Don't just one day decide that your child is dancing to a different tune and start dancing to that tune. Find out what dance they are on. Ask them. Talk to them. Include them. The more you talk and include them, the easier the dance will become. Fortunately, when it comes to parenting, your children are there to help you. What does having your children help you become a good parent look like? To start, how about paying attention? In parenting, lots of time, you have instant feedback, so pay attention. My son did not want a party. My wife knew that before I even asked him why. She pays attention. She knew how Will was and what he was like. I did not. I assumed I knew what Will wanted. Dad, don't assume you know what your children want. We have all done that, but stop assuming. Don't be afraid to ask them. Yes, learning how to dance is hard, but learning how to be a good father doesn't have to be.

Find support. I know that our church has a parenting class every Thursday night. Find somebody to help you learn how to dance your kids' dance. A lot of this just comes down to a willingness to meet your children where they are and being open to listening to them and others who are there to help. It's like this: in my mind, I am a great dancer. When I close my eyes and imagine myself dancing, it is a beautiful thing. I glide across the dance floor, and nobody has ever made dance as beautiful as I have. However, I know that is just a fantasy I have made up. I need help with dance, and you do, too. I needed help understanding my son, and Elisabeth was there to help me. Who do you have who will help you? I promise, if you look for help, it will be there.

Core Values

"Willy was my Foster Dad, Youth Pastor, and High School Football Coach. I remember having to run and do my homework at the same time. He pushed me to be more than I ever thought I could be. I learned what was important in life from Willy."-Nate

Dad, what are you teaching your kids? As I have already said, I grew up with a fantastic example of what a dad should be. I do many things now because my dad modeled them for me, and one of the most striking lessons I ever learned from my father was generosity. It was a core value of his, even if he never said it out loud. Because of the things I saw him do, I knew that generosity was extremely important to his value system. His modeling for me has, in turn, made generosity important to me.

Generosity is defined as *The quality of being kind and generous. "I was overwhelmed by the generosity of friends and neighbors." Synonyms: liberality, lavishness, magnanimity, munificence, openhandedness, free-handedness, unselfishness; kindness, benevolence, altruism, charity, big-heartedness, goodness; literary bounteousness, "the generosity of our host."* ▪ *the quality or fact of being plentiful or large" diners certainly cannot complain about the generosity of portions."* ▪ *abundance, plentifulness, copiousness, lavishness, liberality, largeness, "the generosity of the food portions."* Personally, I like the last one that says the quality or fact of being plentiful or large.

Dads, do you realize that you are larger than life in your kid's eyes? You are the one they look to as an example of everything they do in life. (Moms, I'm not leaving you out. Your kids also look to you, but this is a book for dads). I remember when I was in my early 20s, and my dad was selling my sister's car. He had bought my sister a 1965 Rambler when she was 16 because he wanted her to be safe. If you need to know what a 1965 Rambler is, picture a tank on wheels. It was a fantastic car. She could fit herself and seven friends in it on any given day. It was huge! He was selling it because she had gotten a different car and no longer needed that one. One day, a guy stopped by and was looking at the car.

He told my dad he wanted to buy it, and they began to talk about the car. The man shared that he was trying to buy it and flip it for more money. My dad had no problem with anybody trying to make money, but this particular man was trying to talk my dad down from the $1,500 price. The gentlemen trying to buy the car kept finding fault after fault with the car to make the case for a lower price. Many of the things he complained about were not issues but just little things.

I remember watching this whole thing unfold until, finally, the guy made his offer that was only a small portion of the car's worth. I remember my dad getting so upset. He told the man the car was no longer for sale. The man tried to increase his offer, and my dad just told him no. My dad said he would not sell the car to him, no matter how much he offered. Eventually, the man offered the full price of the car, and I thought my "dad got him." He would sell the car now. My dad politely said the car was no longer for sale and turned and walked into the house. I was shocked, but not as shocked as I would be the following day when a young 18-year-old came asking about the car.

As this kid began to look at the car, he was so excited. He loved the car, and it would be his first car. He asked my dad how much, and my dad told him the car was for sale for $1,500. He said that was a great deal, but he told my dad he didn't have enough money to buy the car outright and asked if he could make payments. As they talked, I remember thinking, no way he'd go for that. He could have gotten full price yesterday but didn't sell the car. I thought this kid was out of luck. I was wrong; they shook hands on a deal that ended up being for one-third of the original price, and he let the kid make payments.

I was shocked! After he left, I asked my dad what that was about. I said, "You could have gotten full price last night, but you practically gave the car away today. What gives?" That was the day I learned one of the greatest lessons about generosity. He said, "Son, it was never about the money. The first guy was trying to make a buck and could afford to pay more than I asked. This kid needs a break. He needs somebody to give him a hand in life. Son, there are more important things than money." That was my dad, always willing to help somebody who needed help.

I know for some of you that the story is so opposite of what you think you should teach your children because our world says that we need to teach them how to be business savvy. We need to teach them the art of the deal, and while I don't disagree with some of that, I do disagree with teaching our children how to make a buck without teaching them the responsibility that the dollar brings.

Some believe the capitalist system we have in the US is the greatest economic system ever created. That may or may not be true, but even if it is true, that system has been perverted and distorted by greed. Fathers must begin to teach their children that we are blessed so that we can be a blessing. God gives to us so we can give to others. Sometimes, making less money in a deal is the right decision if that decision can bless somebody else.

Generosity is a gift my father taught me, and generosity is a gift I hope to teach my children. Fathers, be generous and let your children see you being generous. Sometimes, you are the miracle that somebody has been praying for. That teen needed a miracle. I don't know if he was a Christian, but he received a miracle from my father that day. One of the ways I teach my children about generosity is by demonstrating it. Generosity is not just about finances. Generosity is about giving. Yes, you can give your money, but you can also give your time, compliments, or even a great attitude. Giving comes in all shapes and sizes. To give is to let go of something you possess. Do you have the ability to let go of a compliment? When I am with my children and we are anywhere, I am very mindful of how I address people. I am always very respectful and try to say please and thank you. I knew I had hit this point one day when I was with my daughter, and for whatever reason, I was not in the greatest mood. We were in a diner, and a waitress was helping us. I do not believe I was rude, but I wasn't as nice as usual. After a brief interaction with the waitress, my daughter scolded me for my behavior. I knew it wasn't as bad as she said, but I was happy she knew what was expected. She was learning what generosity looks like.

Opportunities to teach generosity happen to us all the time. Recently, I got a speeding ticket from a California Highway Patrol

Officer. He was on a motorcycle, I was speeding, and I did not see him. My daughter was in the car, and we had the usual interaction you have with a CHP officer. After he handed me the ticket, I said, "Thank you for your service, and be safe, officer." He thanked me and said, "Given our circumstances, that sentiment was very nice."

    I didn't think about my actions until we started pulling away, and my daughter told me, "Dad, you are so nice." I demonstrated generosity of spirit to my daughter that day. I was generous with kindness. The world needs children growing up where generosity becomes standard practice. Capitalism needs generosity. Think about it. If we could replace greed with generosity, our world would be much different. Our capitalistic system in America is great, but greed has hijacked it. It is still a great system, but it is a system that needs to be redirected and redefined. We need to start rewarding generosity and penalizing greed, at least on a social level. Let's begin to celebrate those who are generous and ignore the greedy. Dads, let's do our part and start to change what the world looks like.

Calm in the Storm

"My favorite event was when we all went to Yosemite. In the middle of the night, something turned over our tent; we were screaming for Willy, and sure enough, he came running." - Nate

Dad, do you realize you are supposed to be the calm in the storm? You are the one who is supposed to be who your kids rely on. Dad, God called you to lay your life down for your family. For those fathers who are married, Ephesians 5:25 tells husbands to love their wives the way Christ loved the church and give His life up for the church. Most men would rather read Ephesians 5:22. You know, the one about wives submitting to their husbands, but I have never seen a wife who did not submit to a husband laying his life down for her daily. You are called to die for your wife and your family daily. If that was not upsetting enough, think about this: I have never seen someone die without suffering. You are going to suffer. It is part of the human experience, but how we suffer and deal with it is many times more important than why we suffer. Let's face it: you can do everything right and still suffer. I had to deal with this life lesson when my wife died.

I was going to a counselor. I had things I needed to work through that were related to her death, and one of those things was that even though I had done all the right things, she still died. I was a good husband; I was a faithful husband. I took care of my sick wife. I cleaned, cooked, worked a job, and cared for my kids. I provided everything possible. I was a pastor. I didn't have a secret sin that I was hiding. As far as a dad and a husband go, I was a rock star. I had done everything right, but still, my wife died.

How could I do everything right and have everything go wrong? In this life, we are going to suffer. It is not about what you do and do not do. Yes, sometimes, when you do the wrong things, you have consequences for your actions. If you are a husband and have an affair, don't walk around wondering why your marriage ended. It ended because of some of the choices you made. But sometimes life just happens despite your best efforts.

What do you do then? Do you believe God has a plan for your life? If you do, you must believe that your life is in His hands. The goal in life is not to lead a life free from suffering. That is impossible. The goal should be to develop the character that allows you to handle the suffering you will experience so that you can fulfill the call of Philippians 1:27. "Conduct yourselves in a manner worthy of the gospel of Christ."

Helen Keller said, "Character cannot be developed in ease and quiet. Only through experience of trial and suffering can the soul be strengthened, ambition inspired, and success achieved." I don't think God is that concerned about us being comfortable. I do believe He cares a whole lot about our character. The goal of suffering is found in Romans 5:3-4, "Not only so, but we also glory (rejoice) in our sufferings, because we know that suffering produces perseverance; perseverance, character; and character, hope."

I know it must feel like I am belaboring this point, but understand that how your children learn to deal with and walk through suffering is your responsibility. When you suffer, remember they are watching. I can't tell you how many times I have had men come to me and tell me how I saved their marriages. These were men whom I had never had a conversation with. I never counseled them. I never prayed with them, but when I walked with my wife and children through what became the time of her death, I found out they were watching. One of the men said, "As I watched you, caring for your children, caring for your wife, and continuing to be a man of faith and integrity, I would ask myself how can I be like that guy. I realized I needed to be a better husband."

How do you endure suffering with your faith, integrity, and relationships with your spouse and children strengthened? Hope is my answer. Hope is one of the most powerful forces on the planet. Find hope. Hope will get you to another day. When my wife was dying, I had to find hope every single morning. When I woke up in the morning, I chose to embrace hope. I had a ritual. Every morning when I woke, the first thing I would do was remind myself that today might just be the day of Martha's healing. Today might be the day of a miracle. I don't know what is going on with you, but some of you need to get this concept. Are you suffering financially? Are you suffering from relationships or pain? Whatever it is, realize that today just might be the day of breakthrough. In my case, that day did not come, and at the end of the night, I would begin to prepare myself for another day. I would tell myself that today was not the day of a breakthrough, but tomorrow might be.

You have to stay in a place of hope. Find a place of hope, stay in it, and never leave that place. Keep pushing through. Surround yourself with others who will call you to that place of hope. Those days were dark days when my wife was first diagnosed with Multiple Sclerosis. We needed something to keep us going, so I went and copied and then taped promises from the Bible onto the ceiling of our bedroom. I wanted the first thing we saw in the morning to be the promises of God and the last thing we saw at night to be the promises of God. I have added attachment pages at the end of this book that you can rip out and paste on your walls if this speaks to you. Things like:

God has a plan for my life — Jeremiah 29:11 "For I know the plans I have for you," says the Lord. "They are plans for good and not for disaster, to give you a future and a hope."

God can be trusted — Hebrews 10:23 "Let us hold tightly without wavering to the hope we affirm, for God can be trusted to keep his promise."

God is kind and compassionate — Isaiah 54:10 "Though the mountains be shaken and the hills be removed, yet my unfailing love {kindness} for you will not be shaken, nor my covenant of peace be removed, says the Lord, who has compassion on you."

God designed me for a purpose. — Ephesians 2:10 "For we are God's handiwork, created in Christ Jesus to do good works, which God prepared in advance for us to do."

God loves me deeply, no matter what. — Romans 8:38-39 "For I am convinced that neither death nor life, neither angels nor demons, neither the present nor the future, nor any powers, neither height nor depth, nor anything else in all creation, will be able to separate us from the love of God that is in Christ Jesus our Lord."

God gives me power for my life — 2 Timothy 1:7 "For the Spirit God gave us does not make us timid, but gives us power, love, and self-discipline."

God's presence brings joy — Psalm 16:11 "You make known to me the path of life; you will fill me with joy in your presence, with eternal pleasures at your right hand."
God will fill me to overflowing with hope — Romans 15:13 "May the God of hope fill you with all joy and peace as you trust in him, so that you may overflow with hope by the power of the Holy Spirit."

God will strengthen and help me — Isaiah 41:10 "So do not fear, for I am with you, do not be dismayed, for I am your God. I will strengthen you and help you; I will uphold you with my righteous right hand."

God will give you wisdom –James 1:5 "If any of you lacks wisdom, you should ask God, who gives generously to all without finding fault, and it will be given to you."

God promises you an abundant life — John 10:10 "The thief comes only to steal and kill and destroy. I came that they may have life and have it abundantly."

God's promises never fail. — Joshua 21:45 "Not one of all the Lord's good promises to Israel failed; every one was fulfilled."

God is always good. — Psalm 119:68 "You are good and do good. Teach me your statutes."

God is always with me — Joshua 1:9 "This is my command-be strong and courageous! Do not be afraid or discouraged. For the Lord, your God is with you wherever you go."
God is faithful — Hebrews 10:23 "Let us hold unswervingly to the hope we profess, for he who promised is faithful."

Imagine waking up in the morning, and the very first thing you see is God's promises taped to the ceiling of your room. I wanted us to wake up to God's promises. Why? Because of hope. As I have already said, hope is one of the most potent forces in the universe. Dad, you have to stay in hope during your time of suffering. I am convinced that, often, hope can and will determine the outcome of many situations. And know this, just because the situation, tragedy, or calamity you were going through did not turn out as you expected, it does not mean that your hope was pointless. When we don't see things resolved the way we wanted them to be resolved, it does not mean that God hasn't done His part. What it can mean is that God has something way bigger planned for you than you could ever imagine.

After my wife died, I had options. I could have simply walked away from ministry, the church, and even my faith, and nobody would have blamed me. My wife of 16 years had died a horrible death, and I had two young children. I could have lived on the sympathy of others. Nobody would have blamed me if I had just faded away, but that was not what my kids needed, and it wasn't best for me.

About two weeks after my wife had died, I went to pick up my son from school. He was in the second grade, and his mom, whom he loved more than anybody, had just died. We were driving home, and from the car's back seat, I heard my son say, "Dad, we are going to have a horrible life, aren't we?" I must tell you that anger swelled up in me as I have seldom felt. To be clear, I was not angry with my son. He was an eight-year-old boy who had just lost his mom. I was angry at the enemy who was coming after my son. Hopelessness had set in. Without even a moment of thought, I heard myself saying, "Son, anything but an extraordinary life is unacceptable." I meant what I said, but saying it and meaning it is only part of the picture. Dad, there will be times when you have to take a stand, and that stand may look like you being the encourager in your family's life for years. My children and I faced a tragedy, and there have been daily struggles since that day. They may get easier to deal with, but they are still struggling. Stay committed to being encouraged. Learn how to encourage yourself.

The Greatest Coaching Talk of All Time

Martha and I hid in the dark on a rainy night, waiting for Willy to come home. Once he stepped out of his car, we pelted him with marshmallows.... our laughs and squeals could be heard throughout the neighborhood—what a great memory. - May

The greatest coaching talk of all time. That was the thought going through my mind as I was speaking to my daughter's 3rd grade Hoopsters Basketball team.

That year, I decided to coach my daughter's team. I have years of coaching experience. I coached High School Football for 19 years. I coached on teams that won championships, had players get scholarships to Division One colleges, and even players that went on to play in the NFL. I know how to coach; I am a good coach. At least, that was my thought before volunteering to coach a 3rd-grade girl's basketball team.

It was the first day of practice. I had 12 3rd-grade girls gathered around me, ready to practice. "Ok," I said, "who knows about basketball?" A couple of girls raised their hands. No problem, I can get them coached up. So, I began to explain the game of basketball. I talked about defense, and then I talked about offense. I explained what I wanted to do on both sides of the ball. I talked about ball movement and the importance of finishing your shot. How rebounding is crucial. I even referenced Pat Riley. While I was giving the talk, I literally had the thought going through my mind that this was one of the greatest speeches in my coaching career. I finished and asked, "Any questions?" Almost every girl raised their hand. What is going on? I thought, how can there be questions? Ok, I pointed to a girl and said, "What is your question?" Her response is critical to the point I am about to make. "What is defense, and what is offense? What does that mean?" she asked.

Dad, it doesn't matter how well you think you are doing. If it is not connecting with your children, you need to change your approach. I gave a great coaching speech if I had been talking to high school or college athletes. It was not a great speech for third graders. Some days, your kids will need a hug, and on other days, they may need to hide in the bushes and pelt you with marshmallows. It is your job to know how to reach your kids. On that day, when I was doing the best I thought I could possibly do, I totally missed my target. Are you hitting your target? Are you connecting with your kids? Are you getting down on their level and reaching them where they are?

Your kids are not impressed with how successful you are with your job. You may be the most successful businessman who has ever lived. You may be responsible for millions of dollars, or maybe you're an incredible doctor, lawyer, or pastor. Perhaps you are a cop or a fireman, a real hero of our time. All of that is important, and you should be proud of what you do, but the most important title you will ever receive is the one of daddy. You can be the most important man in the world, but to your kids, you need just to be a dad. All of us who are fathers need to leave our titles at the front door. It's almost like we need a closet to remove our work clothes and put on our daddy clothes. Getting off of work is different for everybody. Some guys can clock out and turn into Daddy without any problems. Others, however, can struggle with this concept. I am one of those fathers. I have a job that I do not clock out of, ever. As I have stated before, I am a pastor; as such, I am sought out by many people daily. For most of my children's life, we have had a Discipleship School with hundreds of students. I know and am known by a lot of people. That fact has brought some disappointment, conflict, and anger to my children. I have not been "present" much of the time when my children have been growing up, which I very much regret. I typically am not someone who regrets much in my life, but not being "present" is one of those things. I have been at most events in my children's lives; however, being there always consisted of a phone in my hand and my mind replying to text messages, phone calls, and general distractions. Dad, do yourself a favor and figure out how to be present. Put the phone on silent and put it away somewhere when you are with your kids. They will notice.

I was first made aware of this about four years ago. I was in the kitchen cooking dinner. As usual, I had other thoughts and things going through my mind. Two of my daughters and one of my sons were present when one of them asked me a question. I replied by saying something like, "That's great." My daughter said, "Dad, stop and listen to me. You didn't hear me. You just blew me off." That caught my attention, and I said, "What do you mean?" She said, "You have a tone when you are not listening to me." I, of course, wanted to defend myself and said, "No, I don't." The other two children jumped in and said, "Yes, you do, Dad. You do this thing when you are not paying attention." I tried to argue, but to be honest, they had busted me, and I had no defense. My children had gotten used to me blowing them off because I had more important things to do. At least, that was the message I was telling them. Men, yes, your jobs are important. Yes, what you do for a living matters, and yes, many people may be relying on you. But our kids have to come first. We must set aside time to make them the center of our world.

I know, even the thought of that can be daunting, but let's take a look at what that really means. It looks different depending on the age of your children. When they are little, it means setting aside some time to just play with them, tuck them in bed, and read them a story. It doesn't take a lot of time, but the time you give needs to be uninterrupted time.

What about as they get older? The older they get, the less contact you are going to have. That is just life, but the older they get, the more you need to be able to listen. Listen to what they are telling you and listen to what they are saying to others when you are around them. Go to their events, and remember to show up. Dad, keep your promise. Don't say you're going if you're going to miss it. Be as involved as you can be. Remember, every child has his or her own unique dance. Figure out what that dance is, and go for it. Remember, you will make mistakes, but just correct and keep going. You can do this!

But how? I am sure some of you are asking that right now. How do I become more present? Start by creating simple rules to follow, and I don't mean house rules for your kids to follow I mean rules for you to follow. Things like when I come home from work I am going to put my phone away. Most of us don't have jobs where we are on call 24-7. Stop acting like you do. You can turn your phone off for a few hours and the world will not end. Show you children that they are more important than work. If your kids are little take time when you get home and play with them. Give them your time. They will notice when daddy has time for them. As your kids get older connection time gets harder and harder but it can be done. I cook dinner. When I am cooking sometime one or more of the kids will be around. That is a great time to put your phone away, turn off the tv and just have conversations. Bottom line when your kids around they should get your undivided time. I know this may feel daunting but you can do it, and I promise you if you do you will not regret it.

Influence

Willy taught me how to be a man. I am a good father today because of the lessons I learned in his house. Mostly, I just watched what he did. - Nate

"G** D*** it," is what I heard from the car's back seat on the way home from church one day. "G** D*** it, G** D*** it," I kept hearing that word. My 3-year-old little angel was in the back seat. What was going on? Was I really hearing that? I turned down the radio so I could be sure I was hearing what I thought I was hearing. I heard it again, although this time it was louder. She must have realized I turned down the music to hear her, and she wanted to make sure that I did. For a moment, I thought maybe I accidentally left Moriah at church and brought home an off-duty drunk sailor. Nope, I looked in the back and saw my sweet little girl, who was as innocent as anybody has ever been. I said, "Moriah, what did you say?" she looked right at me and said, "I left my G** D*** socks on the playground."

There are a lot of excuses that I could make for the language that came out of my 3-yearold's mouth that day. Maybe she heard it on the playground. Perhaps she heard from one of the other kids in church. You know, the ones with the questionable families. Maybe it was the influence of some of the students in our discipleship school. Some of them can be a bad influence. Like I said, I could make excuses for who she learned that language from or where she heard it, but all of that would be a lie. She heard it from me. How do I know that she heard it from me? Because when she said it the last time, she said it with all the enthusiasm she could muster, and she even used the same inflections I used in my voice. She was copying me. I was the bad influence.

Before you judge me, consider this. My wife of 17 years had died. I was a single dad of two little kids and I was thousand of dollars in debt from medical bills. I had lived with the stress of a dying spouse for years. My health was extremely precarious due to the stress I had lived with. I was on a razors edge and doing everything I could to not fall off and take my kids with me. I didn't turn to drugs, alcohol or other destructive things that many people do, but my anger which included my language was out of control. That story you just read is real. My daughter learned that language from me, but that was also a moment where I began too see how my actions were effecting my kids. That day I knew I had to do something different, and I began to make the changes I needed to be in order to be a better dad and a better role model.

Dad, remember your kids are watching EVERYTHING. How you conduct your life matters. What you do and do not do matters. The fact that my daughter heard me say those words is undoubtedly not the end of the world, but if she saw that, what else was she paying attention to? The answer to that is, again, everything. Dad, there are certain things that our children should not be privy to because they are children. I pastor a church. Unfortunately, in a church, people sometimes do horrible things to each other and the pastor. I have been at the end of some horrible attitudes against me over the years of pastoring. I know many pastors who go home and vent with their spouses in front of their children. All that is doing is poisoning your children. Our children do not need to hear all the dirty gossip that we are going through. They will learn soon enough about the hardship of the world.

Not too long ago, our church went through a split. It was a tough time. From the outside, we did a pretty good job of not airing our dirty laundry, and to most people, it seemed like a friendly parting. I will not go into any details of the division because, honestly, they don't matter. Wrong things were done, and wrong things were said. Attitudes were not what they should have been, and the whole thing was just a bummer. Publicly, I did a good job of getting through it, but behind the scenes, I was a mess. I spent time in therapy and felt a sense of betrayal I had not felt in a long time. There was a lot to process. My wife was a strength to me in those times. I thank God for her and her counsel. She has a wisdom that often helps me when making decisions, but even though I would go home and talk with her, I tried very hard not to talk about or process with her when the kids were around. It does help that our youngest are now teenagers who are either gone or in their rooms, but even if that were not the case, I would find a way to have those conversations in private. Why? Because I do not want my kids poisoned by my bad attitudes or others' bad attitudes. Our kids see and hear everything; they will take sides when they listen to problems or conflicts. They will react and turn against those hurting their dad. Don't let that happen. Adult problems should not be placed on children. Dad, conflicts at work should stay at work. Dad, we are responsible for making sure we present the world as a safe place. Sometimes, it is not, but our children do not need to see that until they absolutely have to. They will face a world that is against them soon enough. But let's make sure we keep them in a place of safety as long as we can.

What about when the world around them just erupts? One time, while doing foster care, we lived next to a neighbor who was less than friendly. Okay, actually, he was kinda of a jerk. I am not sure there was anybody in his life who actually liked the man, and that included his family. He was abrasive, rude, and just plain mean. One day, one of our foster sons was out across the street riding his skateboard. He wasn't doing anything wrong. He was minding his own business and just having fun. The neighbor decided he didn't want him riding his skateboard outside and went out and started yelling at him. I heard the commotion and came running. I immediately defended my foster son. It was not okay for this man to be yelling at him. I became very upset and started yelling at the neighbor. My foster son actually had to calm me down. (Side note: I did apologize to my neighbor later, but he wasn't interested in hearing from me.) We went inside, and my foster son had tears in his eyes. I thought the neighbor had hurt his feelings, so I was trying to console him when he said, "You don't get it. I am not crying because he hurt my feelings; I am crying because nobody has ever stood up for me before." He was 16 years old, and nobody in his entire life had ever stood up for him. That is just wrong.

As a father, you have a sacred role in protecting your family. Yes, moms protect too. How else would the "mamma bear" be a thing? But as a father, you need to know that you should be leading the charge when it comes to protecting the family. But let's get real for a moment. Most of us no longer live in places where wild bears, mountain lions, and many other things are likely to attack us. Most of us do not fear our homes being broken into and our children or wives being hurt. So, for this book, I want to focus on protecting our family's spirits. Dad, how you treat your wife, children, and even your pets will set the tone for how they treat others in their lives. Your children are looking to you. You are their example. Many of the kids I have had in my home have had horrible examples of how a father treats his family. They either came from a family where the father completely abandoned them, their father was incarcerated, their father was a drug addict, and or abusive. Many of them never even met their father. These kids had a rough start with the idea of a father. Coming to my house, you could see their hesitation around me. Trust was something I had to earn. It was never just given.

Dad, you have to earn the trust of your children. Some of you have done this already. You have been involved, and you have proven yourself, but some of you reading this have not developed the trust that you need to, and you have some work to do. Trust takes time to build, and trust is not something that you can force into anybody, especially children. All you can do is love them, keep loving them, and never stop loving them. The longer you love them and stay consistent in that love, the more they will trust you.

We had teens on probation living in our homes. Often, they failed. They did things wrong most of the time, but we had made a commitment to loving them. When they failed, it was not the end of the world and overreacting was something we tried never to do. Dad, don't overreact. Remember, you were once a kid, too. You probably used to do a lot of the same things that your kids do. You survived, and they will as well. When your kids fail, that is the best time to love them. Yes, you heard me right. When they fail, that is the time to love them, to really push in with love. Let them know that you love them and you will always love them. If you know you are loved unconditionally, that is a love that never has to be tested.

When I was 18, I walked out of the Christian church and decided it wasn't for me. I had grown up in a church. As I have already told you, my grandfather was a church planter for the Assemblies of God fellowship. I am now ordained with that very same fellowship today. I grew up Assemblies of God: my perception was it was a place that was rule-driven and rewarded those who kept their sins in secret. It was okay to be a sinner as long as no one found out. It was the kind of place where, every week, I felt as if I had to go down and accept Jesus into my heart once again because I just knew I had done something wrong.

I am not sure what a little boy of eight or nine does that is going to send him to hell, but I was sure I had done it. So, every Sunday, I responded to the alter call and got saved all over again. That was the way it was. You got right on Sunday, and then you had to get right again by the next Sunday. After doing that for many years, it started to dawn on me that no matter what I did, I could not live up to the standard that was being presented. When I turned 18, I was done. Doing my best wasn't good enough, and if I was going to go to hell, I might as well have a great time before I go. So I started doing what many 18-year-olds do, whatever I wanted. I am not gonna lie. I did a lot of things I should not have done. I was testing the boundaries of God's love. I was never taught that His love has no ending. I was never taught that His love is unconditional, so in my mind, I was gonna find out how far I could go to get Him to stop loving me. To my surprise, He never stopped, and when I was a junior in college, He really started pouring out His love into my life.

That year, 1987, my college buddies and I decided we would go to Daytona Beach for Spring Break. Yes, Daytona Beach. We went to Daytona, and my roommates had a great time. I, on the other hand, had moments that changed my life. About a month before we went to Daytona, I felt the Lord begin to move on me. (I apologize if you are not a Christian and do not understand what I am saying. This is a real part of my journey, and it is important to the point.) I felt Jesus just begin to tell me how much He loved me. He kept telling me over and over again, I love you. I am proud of you. I kept hearing those phrases. I knew they were from Him because I wasn't gonna say that about myself. At Daytona, that continued, and while my friends were out partying, I was down on the beach by myself, just talking to God. That is where I began to learn about unconditional love. I found a God who loved me even when I did things wrong. I found a God who loved me at my worst moments. That love, that unconditional love, was calling me. I learned what Romans 8:39 means, "No power in the sky above or in the earth below—indeed, nothing in all creation will ever be able to separate us from the love of God that is revealed in Christ Jesus our Lord." I STOPPED TESTING HIS BOUNDARIES once I understood He was gonna love me no matter what. Dad, parents, we have all had these moments with our kids. Sometimes, they are testing the boundaries of our love. Show them that you love them no matter what.

I believe that if we teach our children that we love them unconditionally, they will find the right path. They will find the path they are supposed to travel. Unconditional love means our children never have to wonder about their place in our hearts. They know we will always be there. So yes, when they fail or do something wrong, push into that with love that is neverending. Love is the ultimate act of protecting our children. Love them, protect them.

Times are changing

"My dad is constantly changing. As I've grown, I've looked back at our memories and noticed how much he's changed. My dad is an entirely different person now than when I was 14." - Moriah at 19 yrs old

I love to have dinner around the table with my family. Having the whole family there is a very rare occasion, but two of my daughters still live at home. I enjoy the conversations that sometimes develop. As the kids have gotten older, this happens less and less because they are all busy building their own lives, but every so often, we still get to sit down as a family, have dinner, and talk. What I experience at those dinners is a generation that thinks completely differently than I do. My kids care about people in a way that I was never taught to. They care for all people. They view the Christian Church as a place of hatred and bigotry. They think it is homophobic and a place that is just plain mean to people. They see church members who are calling out their peers and culture but are doing it in a way that screams hate and not love. The church is about to lose an entire generation if it doesn't make some changes. Dad, we have to change our approach with our children. We cannot be part of the problem. We need to approach our kids differently.

My generation played "smear the queer." Most men my age will remember this game. We played it on the playground in front of the teachers. We even had a teacher who helped us play the game as he would throw the ball up higher than any of us could. What was smear the queer, you may ask? Smear the queer was a game where a group of boys would gather around with a football. One boy would throw the ball in the air, and everybody would try to catch it. Whoever caught the ball became the queer and immediately started running. Once someone was identified as queer, meaning he had caught the ball, we all tried to tackle him and pummel him. We tried to "smear the queer."

What a loving game, right? No....it is a horrible game. But can you imagine being an eight or nine-year-old little boy and playing this?

You could not play it in today's world. Anybody involved in that would be dealt with severely. The teacher who threw us the ball would be fired. Heck, any teacher not immediately stopping the game would be fired. The kids on the playground would all be suspended, and it would be a major issue. But in 1973? That was completely acceptable because being queer back then meant you were the Enemy—something to be loathed. When I was in school, nobody came out as part of the LGBTQ+ community. Nobody would dare. If you came out back then, it meant your friends left you, your family left you, and if it was common knowledge, good luck getting a job. Being different was not something you did.

Recently, I read a book called Escaping Enemy Mode by James Wilder and Ray Woolridge. If you have not read this book, I highly recommend it. Both of these authors lay out the case that we are being indoctrinated every day by multiple sources that are trying to get us to consider each other the Enemy. Smear the queer is an enemy-mode game, and although you can no longer play that and get away with it, enemy-mode has crept into every part of our society. It is clear that nations have thrived on enemy mode, the media thrives on enemy mode, and religion has thrived on enemy mode. Much of society has been programmed to accept enemy mode as fact. It is us against them. It doesn't even matter who we are or who they are. We are at odds with each other. Why? To put it simply, Enemy Mode sells. Every year, billions of dollars are made to get people to hate each other. Understand, we live in a better society than in the 1970's. We are way more accepting than ever, but for some people, that has brought a lot of anger and angst. For many people, having others who are different than them is not okay. Their being different is seen as a threat to our existence. The mindset is just another way to continue to see different as the enemy instead of listening and understanding. Instead of having a conversation and finding a middle ground, we just label others with something that makes them our Enemy. Dad, we can't be like the world. We have to show our children a different way.

Our children may have only known a world that is at odds with itself. When our children come home and challenge a norm that is part of your family, do not react like they have just become your Enemy. They are not your Enemy. They are your children. They are saying things, doing things, and challenging our norms because they are just trying to find their way in this really messed up world. What if, when your kids begin to find their own identity, instead of reacting, you begin to listen to them and really hear what they are saying? When my kids and I have dinner together, I hear a generation that really cares for others. To them, accepting others as they are is not liberal or far left, it is being human. It is caring for others. Remember, train your child in ways he/she should go? What if we trained our children to love all? I remember Jesus being pretty good and loving all. He loved the tax collector which back then was just another name for thief and trader to the Jewish people. He loved the prostitutes, the criminals and actually reached out and touched the leper, which was a crime punishable by death. Jesus loved all. When I hear my kids at dinner they sound more like Jesus than what I hear in many Christian circles today. As your children begin to care for and about others, we should support that. We should push into that and not put it in the conflict column. Yes, their values will be different than ours. The LGBTQ+ movement is accepted by my kid's generation. They do not understand why who someone is with or who they are choosing to love is anybody else's business. For those of you who are Christians and want to push back with, "It's what the Bible says, your kids don't care. They are not going to care, and if you continue to treat it like a Biblical deal breaker they are going to continue to pull away from our churches as fast as they can. This has already happened. When was the last time a denomination reported actual growth? You can't think of one, and neither can I. Many denominations have hopped on board with enemy mode and promoted hate. I don't think they actually mean to promote hate, but that is exactly what is happening. Our kids care more about loving people than what the Bible does or does not actually say.

Do you realize that pre-1965, it was commonplace for Christians to hate Jews? Why do you think Hitler had such an easy time convincing a nation that the final solution was the right thing to do? The Christian church was complacent when it came to the Holocaust. David P Gushee, in his book *Changing Our Mind*, lays out the case that the hatred of Jews was a fundamental belief in Christendom for the last two thousand years. The church taught that the Jews were an evil people. A people who sided with Satan. One of the scriptures used was from John 8:44 - "You are of your father the devil, and your will is to do your father's desires." For centuries in Christianity, it was taken that Jews were the children of the devil. Pious kids would look for horns on the Jewish children in school. Christian children would call Jewish children Christ Killer. Matthew 27:25 - "His blood be on us and our children." That is what the Jews yelled out as Pilate washed his hands, saying, "I am innocent of this man's blood," he said. "It is your responsibility!" Jews were to be hated, mocked, and ostracized from civilization. They were the Christ killers. Where did this hate come from? You guessed it, the Bible, of course.

I could go on and on about ways the Bible has been misrepresented, but I will stop here. I hope you get the picture. The Bible is not supposed to be used as a club, and when it has been, the outcome has almost always been horrible.

Instead of creating enemy mode, what if we just let people be who they want to be? What if we let our children find the ways THEY are supposed to go? Dad, remember, our ways are not their ways. Let's stop forcing ourselves on them. As you know already, I am a Christian, and I am a pastor. It is my job to lead and run our church. I have chosen the path of love, grace, and patience. I have people coming to my church from all walks of life. All are accepted. Everybody is welcome. The pushback I get is never from the community. The pushback I get is only from other Christians who cannot understand why I am not operating in enemy mode. I have often been told that I have too much grace for people. They say I do not preach the whole message of Jesus. I disagree with that take. There are a lot of things in this world and certainly in the next world to come that I do not know. But I am willing to bet the house on this one thing. One day, I will stand before my God to give an account of my life. I cannot imagine any scenarios where I will hear the following words, "Willy, you loved too much, Willy, you had too much grace for people."

Dad, what if we started loving our children unconditionally? What if we started showing grace to them, grace that is even beyond what they deserve? What if we started to father like the example that Jesus gave us regarding love? What if when our children do something, say something, or act in a way that is opposite of us, we begin to embrace them on a greater level? I think if we learn to love our children in this way, our children will turn out better than we ever expected. Love conquers all! Times have changed, and if we are going to reach our children, we are going to have to change with them.

But what if your child is gay? I am not gonna lie. The thought of that sentence coming out of the mouth of one of my children brought fear to me for many years. It still does, but for many different reasons than it did when my oldest said those words to me twenty-plus years ago. I didn't handle her proclamation very well. As I look back on that time, I am disappointed, embarrassed, and ashamed of the way I treated my daughter. At the time, I was doing what my church background had taught me to do. The church had taught and, therefore, I had taught that homosexuality is a sin and not just a sin but the worst sin. According to Leviticus 18:22, it is an abomination. Of course, Exodus 21:17 says whoever curses his mother or father should be put to death, so maybe we should not try to institute Old Testament law in the modern-day world. But, when it came to homosexuality, there was no pulling punches. There was simply no room for a homosexual in the Christian church.

I was afraid. I was afraid that my daughter was lost and going to hell, but I am ashamed to admit, that I was also afraid for my reputation, career, and standing in the Christian community. I was afraid for me. I was afraid of what the "shame" of my daughter being gay would mean for me. I was in ministry, I was a youth pastor, and I was worried I was going to lose my job. Looking back now, I realize how poorly I handled that situation. I suspect many people have made or are still making those kinds of mistakes when their children come out as being part of the LGBTQ+ community. It is truly one of the most disappointing things I have ever done as a father. Almost thirty years later, the thought of one of my other children making that proclamation still brings fear to me, but now it is for a much different reason.

I am no longer afraid of one of them being gay for the same reason above. Now, after being in ministry for over 30 years, losing my job does not carry the same weight it carried as a young pastor. I am not afraid for my reputation, or standing in the Christian church; heck, I have come to realize that none of those things actually matter. I am still terrified of one of my children or grandchildren making that proclamation, but now I am afraid for one of them being part of the LGBTQ+ community because I know they will have to grow up in a world that is filled with hate.

The world has come a long way since I played smear the queer on the playground, but still, there is much that needs to change. Having a gay child is only one of the many fears a parent faces today. One of my daughters is dating a young man of color. That scares me, and it scares me a lot. To be clear, I am not scared because he is a man of color. He is an amazing guy. I have known him for many years, and I love him dearly. If this relationship works out and my daughter marries him, I will be proud to call him my son, but there are ignorant people in the world who do hate-filled things. People who believe that mixed relationships are wrong. The thought of my kids being different and, therefore, having a bullseye painted on them brings me fear. I think any good parent has those same types of fears. I know, as a white middle-class man, that kind of fear is something I have not ever had to face. I have never before been afraid for my children because of the color of their skin or, in the case of my daughter, because of the skin color of someone she has chosen to date.

I have very dear friends who are men of color. I have heard them tell me how they have had to have the talk with their kids and grandkids. What's the talk? If you asked that, you probably are not a person of color. The talk is about what to do when the police pull you over and how you handle yourself so you do not get shot. Hands-on the steering wheel, don't reach for anything unless asked to do so. Move slow, speak respectfully, things of that nature. I have never thought about having to sit my kids down and tell them about these things. But people of color do. Many parents reading this have lived with this kind of fear concerning their children their entire lives. We live in a hate-filled world, and being different brings out that hate.

What do you do if your child is part of the LBGTQ+ community? LOVE THEM. Love them, love them, love them. Don't let anyone or anything stop you from loving them. Don't let your family, friends, church, or pastor tell you anything different. Your LGBTQ+ child is not broken. Treat them like you would a straight kid, but maybe even love them a little more loudly. The world is cruel and mean. You will have to compensate for that cruelty. Statistics tell me that three to five percent of the parents reading this have children who are part of the LGBTQ+ community. This holds true for Christian parents and non-Christian parents. If you are a parent of a child who is part of the LGBTQ+ community, they need you. Dad, your son or daughter needs you. He/she/they desperately need you. If you are part of a church or community that tells you your child is broken, leave that church or community. Find some other church or community that will accept them. They are your priority. God gave them to you.

What about my oldest daughter? Being gay for her was only a temporary. Since then, she has been married and has three children, one of whom she just adopted. They are my grandkids, whom I love very much. The way I reacted caused a real problem for our relationship. We are patching things together after many years, but it is still a work in progress. I wish I had handled things differently. Dad, don't do what I did.

Legacy

Willy and Martha, through love, taught me to forgive, receive love, accept punishment, experience forgiveness, and learn about the Lord. - May

Fathers, what will your legacy be? Will it be in your home, your cars, your boats, motorcycles, or all the toys you have accumulated, or will your legacy be in something much different? Dad, it is time to start living in a manner that gives your children something to remember you by. As I stated earlier, my father has now passed, but he left a legacy that will forever shape and change the course of our family history. My dad grew up in a house where my grandfather was a World War II Hero. He was part of the Greatest Generation. My grandfather made a great soldier but not a great father. He was awarded the Purple Heart and was responsible for saving countless lives. At times, he was a larger-than-life figure and looked upon as a man's man.

I remember being a little kid in my grandfather's presence, and he still had an air of greatness about him. Unfortunately, being a great soldier didn't translate to being a great father. For many reasons, I have already stated, my aunt, uncles, and dad grew up in an environment much different than my own. Alcohol, drugs, and sex were common in life with the Bowles kids. My dad put a stop to all of that, and I am who I am today because of what he did.

Dad, what do you need to change to be the man you are supposed to be? What do you need to change to be the dad you are supposed to be? Let's be clear: we live in a world that has bought into a lie that says none of us need to change and that we are fine just the way we are. That is a lie. I don't know anybody that is fine, just the way they are. We all need to change. Have the courage to change. Have the courage to do whatever it is that you need to do to be a better person. The last chapter of this book is written by a friend of mine, John Withers. John is a Marriage and Family Therapist and a Pastor in South San Fransisco. I asked John to write a chapter in this book to give anybody reading this tools for change. You can do it. You can change. Use the tools John has written about, and then find some others who will help you. As it is with the Marlboro man, it should not be with us. We are not supposed to be an island. Find others and find community. Here is John.

When You Are Ready For a Change, Change will Be Ready For You

John A. Withers April 16, 2024

There have been many books written to describe manhood and fatherhood and what it supposed to look like, act like and feel like, but in my humble opinion, fatherhood is measure in so many more forms especially emotional, mental and to say the least, but most important, the spiritual component. Before I dive into some of the nitty gritty of this subject, allow me a few moments to tell you a little bit about who I am and where I came from and the one who is still working on himself through the grace of God. Ephesians 2:8-9 For by grace you have been saved through faith. And this is not your own doing; it is the gift of God, not a result of works, so that no one may boast.

I grew up in a black family in the small country town of Pelham, North Carolina with a father and mother and five other siblings, me being the fourth child out of six. It was a harsh and difficult time to grow up. Those times were difficult not only at home but also in our society as a whole and believe me all those circumstances and situations can mold a child's emotional, mental, and spiritual condition. I'm a product of the 50's in the Jim Crow days, whereby schools were not integrated, and racism was progressively increasing. Back then we had labels (color people and white people for everything). And I mean everything. Water fountains, schools and you name it, including restaurants where we had to be served outside rather than coming to sit down and eat inside. I vividly remember that an all-white school was less than three miles from our home, and colored kids could not attend but had to bus miles to get to our destination for colored schools. Ironically, we were never bittered about most circumstance and situations—it was a part of that lifestyle during that season.

Something that many of us overlook is the emotional dysfunctionalities that generally occurs when a child grows up and learns to emulate their parents' behavior…good, bad, and indifferent. Outside of the home, school and nearby friends, notwithstanding television, these influences are the only true examples children have, especially growing up in rural conditions whereby people don't have the luxury of having the simplicities of things in life that are readily available, such as medical, food, even public transportation. For me personally, we did not have running water in our home. Our idea of running water was running down in the bottom of the woods with two one-gallon buckets to be filled from spring water that was encased in concrete 2x2x2 feet, never knowing where that water came from, but it was always clean and refreshing and no one ever got sick. Secondly, if we did not have indoor running water, it was obvious we did not have an indoor bathroom, we had an out-house. If you have never heard of an out-house, you really have had a good life. It's a toilet outside with a hole in the ground about five feet wide and six to eight feet deep. The good thing, it was a little house built to take care of your business outside. I'm grateful that my brother and I only dug that hole once in our lifetime to move that toilet. Not a pretty sight to say the least.

All these emotions play on an impressible young mind during those early years. The most fortunate thing was we were not alone…our nearby neighbors were just as poor as we were, and yet no one begged the difference. We were all the same. Therefore, when we grew up to be adults and parents, we parented the way our parents parented us. One of the worst-case scenarios was when an individual had thoughts that his or her parents were right in everything they said and did, and then they realize that their parents could have been wrong, now they are left to stay in the same state of mind or to relearn what they had been taught and relearn something that is more conducive to their well-being. This is the most difficult change to occur because one must come to grips with the fact that if they do not have a strong will to change, they are bound to remain the same and repeat some or all their parents' setbacks. Notice, I did not call them failures because I realized that did the best they could with what they had, and I would not exchange some of those learning experiences for anything in the world. Though they were tough and challenging times, it helped shape and mold the man that I am today.

My father fathered the way he was fathered, and when I had children, I began to father my children the way my father fathered me. Unemotional, disconnected, angry and bottled up. When I think of the term bottle-up, it reminds me of anger turned outside in. Anger is a healthy human reaction, when it is done right, but it was never meant for the brain to keep it any longer than three to five minutes. Wonder than that and the brain goes into a rage and begins snapping the neurons. Interneurons are neural intermediaries found in your brain and spinal cord. They're the most common type of neuron. They carry signals from sensory neurons and other interneurons to motor neurons and other interneurons. Often, they form complex circuits that help you to react to external stimuli. This is important because these tissues are soft tissues and when the brain is fused with anger our heart rate tremendously increases and then there is a possibility of flooding our brain and losing control altogether. That's when we can hurt someone or ourselves or even both. God gave us a self-soothing mechanism in our brain to be able to talk our self off the ledge. Those with healthy brains have been trained by a healthy systematic family, those who haven't had the privilege to inherit that trait, no sweat: it's there, one just has to exercise that part of the brain. The brain is like a muscle, the more you use it, the more beneficial it becomes to you and the likely hood of keeping your marbles upstairs in check. The great thing is that the human brain continues to grow and expand at any age if you are willing to continue to learn and stimulate it.

Marian Diamond was an American neuroscientist. She and her team were the first to publish evidence that the brain can change with experience and improve with enrichment, and idea now called neuroplasticity. She was a professor of anatomy at the University of California, Berkeley. She said, "We must challenge the brain, It gets bored; we know that well." She went on to say that it may take the older brain longer to respond, but change does happen. In her opinion, people would be wise to think of their brain as a muscle. Left in isolation, evidence shows that the brain begins to shrink and shut down. One of the best mental exercises is learning something or doing something you have not done before. Bottom-line, use it or lose it. I plan on keeping mine.

I have heard that growth only happens when you place yourself in uncomfortable situations or circumstances; however, sometimes life will feel out of control, or we simply don't have control when it comes to situations or circumstances, and especially other people, but we do have control over ourselves. We will always have a choice over how we react. The older I get, the more dominion I have over my thoughts, behavior, and responses and that lets me know I'm growing.

When I was kid in school, if I did anything wrong in class I got spanked from the teacher with a padder (a two-inch thick meat cutting block of wood about 18 inches long with a handle). Then the teacher would write a note to my parents and seal it in an envelope to tell them how bad I was in class. I would hand the note to my mom; now before you think I was brainless, I thought about not giving the note to my mom, but a spanking delayed is worse than the spanking on time. So, my mom would spank me again. Follow-up with my dad coming from work and he would beat me for the third time. These were times I wished I was white kid because white kids had time outs at home. If they acted out little Johnny or Susan would sit in the corner facing the wall. Our idea of time out was when my mom and dad gotbtired of beating us while we were running away from them—everybody stopped for a few moments to rest. I simply could not ever understand how a child could get three beatings for one wrong mistake. It was these awful things that we dealt with emotionally and mentally. I am amazed of how life comes to full circle. I'm so proud of my daughters and their spouses, they have never touched their kids in anger but take the time to help them self-sooth. They are changing the trajectory of those kids' life and breaking more generational curses, and for that, I am extremely grateful.

My father had ways of showing his love without telling us he loved us. In my opinion, telling while showing sure would have been the best scenario for me. What I learned from that is I could not change the past, but I could alter the future by changing myself and stoping myself from being being so angry with the past. But I too have made my share of mistakes. I learned as I went, and I grew up while my kids were growing up. I learned how to apologize to my children when I was wrong, and man did I gain a lot of brownie points from that. I remember my father aligning all his children in a row and outlining who was going to become what, when, and where. I came from a line of military men in my family and my brothers follow suit. Although I was never in the military, I was a soldier in my father's army. I was that child that listened for the most part and followed orders. My military brothers often told me that I would have made the best soldier because I stayed the course and followed through. When my dad said I was going to go to school to become a barber because as a kid I was good at cutting hair, that's what I did—I went to barber school and did that for some years until I realize one day that it was not what I wanted to do for the rest of my life. I later realized I had a call of God on my life, and went into a phase of avoiding that at all costs. Preacher. Pastor. I don't think so, but God has a way of bringing us around to see His way.

I realize I had to make some radical changes in my life and my thought processes had and will continue to be challenged to make me a well-round individual for the glory of God. Albert Einstein once stated the following: "If someone spent fifteen minutes a day learning something new, in a year he would be an expert." I wanted to change my life in order to break generational curses. That change could only take place through the saving grace of Jesus. I was the first person in my family to go to college. For ten years out of twelve straight years I worked a fulltime job, raising a family, pastoring a church, having a small business, and completing an undergrad degree in English Literature with minor in Speech and Communication. Two weeks after graduation I was working on my MDiv. a Master of Divinity in Theology at Fuller's Theological Seminary, which took me five years to complete. Two weeks after that was I was in another master's program at Santa Clara University where I graduated with a Counseling Psychology degree. I said this to not boast, because that's what I'm not about, but to help you understand this little country farm boy, had just enough understanding to know it would be up to me to make the choices to change my life as well as my family. Now I have two daughters who both hold master's degrees and who once told me if they had not seen me going to school, they probably would have not gone either.

I have read in medical journals that a child's personality is 80% developed between the ages of three to five. That is a frightening thought considering the stress levels of new parents, whether young or older, especially if economic conditions aren't ideal.

Here's something to consider: One hot summer day in July about 1963 when the temperatures had surpassed 95 degrees and the humidity was off the chart, my father decided to take his family to the "Whataburger" restaurant in Danville to have a burger and soda. We lived less than five minutes from the Virginia state line before we entered Danville, Virginia. At that time, "color folks" wasn't allowed inside restaurants. Food had to be ordered from a little teenage white girl on roller skates and she would take the order back inside the cool air conditioned restaurant and wait until the order was ready before she came back outside. At that time there were four of us kids, and I was the baby. I will never forget that defining moment of what my father did. He got out of his car and said, "I am going into this restaurant because this is not right to have us burning up in this heat and it is wrong." He was wanting to take all his kids in there with him, but my mother stopped him from doing that. She begged him to stay in the car, but he insisted and went in. Me being the baby, I jumped out and went in with him. The air conditioning felt so good that I just wanted to stay there. All the white people that were inside stood up and called my daddy derogatory names, telling us to get outside now! But he refused to move and so they called the cops and had him arrested. Darned, the brother didn't even get a chance to eat the burger and drink the soda. I ran back to the car. My dad spent three days in the county jail for that stunt. My mom on the other hand had to call our next-door neighbors who happen to have a "party line phone" to come and pick us up. Now a party line phone line for those who are not familiar with that terminology consisted of when multiple people sharing the same phone line. If they decided to stay on the phone while you talked, they heard your whole conversation. Nothing was secret.

My dad was never a man with many words, but when he spoke, we felt the thunder, some times good and some times bad. He worked two jobs all his life, one as a hospital orderly and the other as a sharecropper.

He said, "there are good people and there are some people that aren't so good. But never judge a man by the color of his skin because there are good and bad regardless of who they are." That little piece of information has stayed with me all my life and helped me to have a sound mind and clear understanding of people's character and not make decisions based on the color of someone's skin but who they were as a person.

My dad taught us how to work and whenever we made a commitment to anyone, we were to see it through because our word was our bond. Perhaps that's why no one on my father's side of the family has had a divorce for over a 100 hundred years. Even if the thought came to my mind, I would immediately reject it because of the influence my father had on us all. All my siblings that were married are still married to this day. I look at my father as a man's man. But he certainly had his faults. He had a mean side to him that would come out when he and his friends got together on Saturday night and raised hell. A few nights in jail fighting with his buddies and an acute heart attack made him eventually settle down.

When I look back and take a step forward, I realize healing is a gradual process, and it's okay to seek professional guidance. It is even better when you have a spouse or someone who can speak the truth into your life, provided you are willing to receive it. My wife would speak to me with a gentle spirit and tell me I may need some assistance and I'm so grateful that she spoke into my soul and told me things that I did not want to hear but needed to hear. One of my requirements when I was in grad school was to receive counseling. It taught me how to be mindful and to stay present and avoid getting caught in past trauma. I actually had to reparent myself by treating myself with kindness and self-compassion. I had to find safe people in my life, and people who were and are better than me in so many different facets of life. This is not a form of insecurity, it's a form of being honest with yourself because everyone has something to offer Proverbs 27:17 As iron sharpens iron, So a man sharpens the countenance of his friend. You have the power to transform your family legacy and create a healthier future for yourself. Its not an easy process and may even come with some trial and error.

I had to reject the idea that vulnerability is a sign of weakness. Real strength lies in acknowledging and processing emotions. Daddy issues also known as "Father Complex," refers to mental and emotional issues that arise due to an unhealthy, strained, toxic, or absent relationship with one's biological father during childhood. These issues can affect a person's mindset, attitude, personality, career choices, and intimate relationships in adulthood, and it's real. It's up to you to make it better or worse. I knew little about my father mentally and emotionally and only some spiritually. However, I loved him and I still do to this day. I develop a greater appreciation the older I get. I do understand that unresolved anger can affect our relationships, including marriages, leading to explosive tempers and abusive behavior. I also understand that I'm not responsible for everything that has happened. If I can get my mental state aligned with my spiritual state, then most of my problems will dissipate. Ultimately my goal is to learn to love as Christ loves me. That is enough for all of us to reach for.

Confessions of a Single Parent (Just for fun!)

Single dad, single mom, this section is for you. I was a single dad for five years. My children were 2 and 8 when I first became a single Dad; believe me, I understand that sometimes you do whatever you must do just to get to the next day.

Confession #1 - If you have ever gone to Target to buy socks and underwear for your children so that you don't have to do laundry, you might be a single parent.

Confession #2: If you have ever convinced your 6-year-old that opposite sock day really does exist because you couldn't find a matching pair, you might be a single parent.

Confession #3: If you have ever taken dirty laundry and thrown it in the dryer to "freshen it up," you might be a single parent.

Confession #4 - If dinner four nights in a row consists of Dyno Bites (frozen chicken nuggets in the form of Dinosaurs) and you consider that good home cooking, you might be a single parent.

Confessions #5: If you have ever accidentally left your son at school for two hours on his birthday because you forgot it was an early day schedule and you were running last-minute errands for his birthday, you might be a single parent.

Confessions #6: If you have ever had to go sleep on the couch because your kids have crowded you out of your bed, you might be a single parent.

Confession #7: If you have ever made up an excuse for you kids to stay home from school just because you were to tired to get out of bed, you might be a single parent.

Confession #8: If you have ever put your two year old in her car seat and then put her in the "prayer closet" so she could or would go to sleep because you were just at the end of your rope, you might be a single parent.

Confession #9: If you have ever pulled into your driveway and just sat in your car for an hour because you knew the baby sitter had your kids and you just couldn't face them, you might be a single parent.

Confession #10: If you have ever responded to your child's question, "Dad, what does sex mean?" By, "It means I will beat your ass if you ask me that again." Because the thought of having to answer that seemed so impossible, you just wanted it to go away. You might be a single parent.

Encouragement

Now David was greatly distressed, for the people spoke of stoning him because the soul of all the people was grieved, every man for his sons and his daughters. But David strengthened himself in the LORD his God. I Samuel 30:6-8

David was in a rough spot. While David and his warriors were away, the enemy came into their camp and took everything and everyone: their wives, children, and all of their possessions. Not only had David lost everything he had and everyone he loved, but his men blamed him and were ready to kill him. Fortunately for all his men and his people, David was a leader and knew what to do. "David encouraged himself in the LORD his God." After he encouraged himself, the story went on. David leads his men, rescues everybody, and takes all his enemy's possessions. That's right; David and his men end up getting all of their people and stuff back and plundering all their enemies' stuff. All because David knew how to strengthen himself. If I have learned anything in my 58 years, it is this: breakthrough often comes right after the darkest moments.

You may be in a rough spot and need to encourage yourself. It's the same thing I did when I taped words of encouragement all over our bedroom ceiling when my wife was dying. That one act helped more than I could have ever imagined. No, my wife did not get better physically, but both of us got a lot better emotionally and spiritually. We had hope. Hope is powerful. It is one of the most powerful things on the planet. Encourage yourself. Find hope. Look for it. Search it out, and don't stop searching until you find it. The following pages will help you in your hope journey.

Peace and Joy, Willy

Life is about to explode with abundance. "The thief comes only to steal and kill and destroy. I came that they may have life and have it abundantly."

John 10:10

God is good.

"You are good and do good. Teach me your statutes."

Psalm 119:68

God is faithful

"Let us hold unswervingly to the hope we profess, for he who promised is faithful."

Hebrews 10:23

God will give you wisdom

"If any of you lacks wisdom, you should ask God, who gives generously to all without and it will be given to you."

James 1:5

God is always with me

"This is my command—be strong and courageous! Do not be afraid or discouraged. For the Lord, your God is with you wherever you go."

Joshua 1:9

You are loved!

POP Fathering in a modern-day world

Peace surrounds you

WILLY BOWLES

Joy is upon you

God loves me deeply, no matter what.

"For I am convinced that neither death nor life, neither angels nor demons, neither the present nor the future, nor any powers, neither height nor depth, nor anything else in all creation, will be able to separate us from the love of God that is in Christ Jesus our Lord."

Romans 8:38-39

God has a plan for my life!

"For I know the plans I have for you," says the Lord. "They are plans for good and not for disaster, to give you a future and a hope."

Jeremiah 29:11

God can be trusted!

"Let us hold tightly without wavering to the hope we affirm, for God can be trusted to keep his promise." Hebrews 10:23

God is kind and compassionate

"Though the mountains be shaken and the hills be removed, yet my unfailing love {kindness} for you will not be shaken, nor my covenant of peace be removed, says the Lord, who has compassion on you."

Isaiah 54:10

God designed me for a purpose!

"For we are God's handiwork, created in Christ Jesus to do good works, which God prepared in advance for us to do."

Ephesians 2:10

God is with you.

"So do not fear, for I am with you, do not be dismayed, for I am your God. I will strengthen you and help you; I will uphold you with my righteous right hand."

Isaiah 41:10

God gives me power for my life

"For the Spirit God gave us does not make us timid, but gives us power, love, and self-discipline."

Timothy 1:7

Special Thanks

Elisabeth, marrying you 11 years ago was one of the best decisions of my life. You have encouraged me to keep writing and supported me every step of the way, but we both know you did way more than that. Thank you for the many hours you spent editing all the previous pages. You have taught me how to be a better writer. By now, you can quote most of the book from memory. You are one of the most intelligent people I know, and this book would not exist if you hadn't made all the changes you made. Thank you for EVERYTHING! Love you forever, Willy

Also, to Dave Brown and Joe McCasland. You both are amazing artists, and I love that your artwork is in my book. You guys rock!

Willy Bowles is the Senior Leader of Lifehouse Humboldt. Lifehouse is a church in Eureka, in the heart of Humboldt County, California. Willy has been the Senior Pastor of Lifehouse since 2003. He is also an Executive Presbyter for the Northern California & Nevada District of the Assemblies of God fellowship. Along with being a Senior Pastor and Executive Presbyter he is also a Certified Mental Health Coach licensed by the American Association of Christian Counselors. Willy founded and was the Director of Bethel  School of Supernatural Discipleship, the sister school to BSSM in Redding, CA. Founded In 2001, BSSD had hundreds of students, all under the direct supervision of Willy and his team. He also founded Homes of Refuge Group Home, where he received the Lt. Governor's Award for outstanding work with California's youth. Willy coached High School Football for over 19 years, where he coached numerous championship teams and players who had careers in the NFL.

Willy and his first wife Martha were foster parents for 11 years, and during that time, they had over a hundred teenagers who would eventually pass through their home. Most of those teens in Willy and Martha's home were on probation. After a long battle with MS, Martha passed away in 2008. Willy was a single parent for five years until he met and married his amazing wife, Elisabeth. Willy and Elisabeth have been married for over ten years. Together, Willy and Elisabeth have five kids and three grandkids. Ruth, Connor, Will, Moriah, and Hannah. The grandkids are Martha, Ella, and Grayson. They also have two dogs, Ollie and Sissy.

Made in the USA
Middletown, DE
14 June 2024

55750776R00064